SAT Sentence Completion Workbook

Erica L. Meltzer

Table of Contents

Introduction to Sentence Completions

For many test-takers, the vocabulary portion of the SAT is one of the most daunting aspects of the test. Although sentence completions comprise less than one-third of the total questions on the Critical Reading section, they test words that many high school students will never have encountered before.

One of the most important things to understand, however, is that the SAT is not a conventional vocabulary test – that is, what's tested is the ability to use the information you do have to figure out the information you don't have, and to make reasonable conjectures based on a careful and logical process of elimination. The ability to memorize hundreds or thousands of words is ultimately just as important as being able to use contextual clues and a basic knowledge of roots to make educated guesses about the meanings of unfamiliar words.

Believe it or not, the College Board does not intend for people to spend huge amounts of time trying to memorize 5,000 words; that's just not what the test is about. (If you're not a native English speaker or come from a home where the primary language spoken is not English, that's a little different, however.) Some of the most challenging questions actually test second or third meanings of very common words – words like "bent" and "conviction," which would be highly unlikely to appear on any SAT vocabulary list because they run exactly counter to most people's notion of what an "SAT word" is.

This is in no way to suggest that you do not need to study vocabulary: many of the core group of 300 or so "hard" words tested will in fact be unfamiliar and have the potential to cost you quite a few points, especially if you're getting most of the passage-based questions right. You need to put in the time and learn them.

The other reason that studying vocabulary is so important is that it will improve your comprehension of both the passages and the answer choices as well. Many of the same words tested in the sentence completions will also appear in the passages themselves. Furthermore, a number of passage-based questions do test vocabulary, some indirectly and some quite directly. Occasionally, all of the answer choices to a passage-based question will consist of SAT vocabulary words – if you don't know the meaning of the words, you simply can't answer the question with any degree of certainty.

Overview of Sentence Completions

Sentence completions appear at the beginning of each Critical Reading section. Each sentence contains either one or two blanks accompanied by five answer choices, all of which will be in the correct form (e.g. all verbs or all adjectives) necessary to complete the sentence in a grammatically correct manner.

Although the number per Critical Reading section and even the overall number of sentence completions per test can fluctuate slightly, the **most common** configuration is as follows:

-First Critical Reading section = 8 sentence completions

-Second Critical Reading section = 5 sentence completions

-Third Critical Reading section = 6 sentence completions

Each set of sentence completions is arranged in order of least to most difficult, but the difficulty is not cumulative from section to section. In other words, #8, the last sentence completions of the first Critical Reading section may have a difficulty level of 5 (most difficult), but the first sentence completion of the next Critical Reading section will start over at a difficulty level of 1.

Since memorizing vocabulary for the SAT is a rite of passage and one of the most talked-about aspects of the test, many students are surprised to discover that the SAT contains only about 20 sentence completions out of 67 questions. As a result, they sometimes underestimate the impact it can have on their score, particularly at the higher end. A test-taker who misses two vocabulary questions per section on each of three Critical Reading section can generally only miss *one* additional Critical Reading question on the entire test and still score above 700. As a result, anyone who does not already possess an exceptional vocabulary and wants to obtain a high Critical Reading score should expect to spend a significant amount of time learning words likely to appear on the SAT.

There is no "best" way to study vocabulary. Some people find pre-made flashcards helpful; others learn by writing definitions. Regardless of preferences, you should plan to spend at least 15 minutes or so per day reading a challenging contemporary publication (e.g. *The Economist*, *The New York Times*) and keep a running list of unfamiliar vocabulary words and their definitions. As a general rule, any word whose meaning you are not 100% certain of, or that you cannot define out of context, should be looked up and written down.

Types of Sentence Completions

Sentence completions test vocabulary in two ways: the first kind simply requires you to use contextual clues to determine meaning. While the words themselves may be challenging, the intended meaning is fairly clear. For example:

> Elvis Presley is regarded as one of the most important figures in twentieth-century popular music because of his unusually ------- repertory, <u>which encompassed genres ranging from country to pop ballads and blues.</u>

(A) rebellious
(B) noxious
(C) eclectic
(D) impulsive
(E) somber

The phrase "which encompassed genres ranging from country to pop ballads and blues," tells us that we're looking for a word that means "containing lots of different types of things." The answer is (C) because that's exactly what "eclectic" means. This is a medium-level question since it's fairly straightforward but contains some choices that many high school students are unlikely to know (*noxious*, *eclectic*, and *somber*).

The second type of sentence completion is less about the words and more about the logic of the sentence itself. Often, these types of questions will contain **negations** so that you will be looking for a word that means the *opposite* of the idea being conveyed.

For example:

> Because migrant workers experience a variety of cultures
> and see the world from ------- cultural perspectives, they
> are often capable of identifying opportunities easily overlooked
> by their **less** ------- counterparts.

   (A) eclectic . . provincial
   (B) diverse . . ambivalent
   (C) heterogeneous . . astute
   (D) myriad . . cosmopolitan
   (E) restricted . . pragmatic

For the first blank, the phrase "variety" of cultures suggests that the correct word means "many," but that only gets rid of (E). The second part of the sentence tells us that these workers are fortunate because they can spot opportunities that people who *haven't* experienced a variety of cultures would miss. But the word *less* means that the word in the blank must mean the **opposite** of *haven't experienced a variety of cultures*. In other words, the right answer means *have experienced a variety of cultures*. Which leaves only (D), cosmopolitan.

Occasionally, the most difficult questions will test the ability to follow the logic of a sentence as well as knowledge of advanced vocabulary, but the majority involve only one skill.

How to Work Through Sentence Completions

As is true for everything on the SAT, working carefully and systematically through sentence completions is the key to correctly answering every question that you are capable of correctly answering. I repeat: it does not matter how strong a vocabulary you have. Working this way ensures that you will not overlook crucial information or make careless errors. The scantron does not care whether you knew the answer – it just scores what you put down.

1) Identify and mark key words or phrases

Sentences will always contain built-in clues to either the definition of one or both words, or to the relationship between the words. Circle/underline or otherwise mark them so you know what to pay attention to. For a discussion of how to identify key words, see the following page.

2) Plug in your own words

If you do this and one of the words is contained in an answer choice, check it **first**. There's no guarantee that it'll be right, but when it is, you can save yourself a lot of time. If you have more information about the second blank, start with it instead.

You should spend **no more than a couple of seconds** attempting to fill in your own word. It doesn't matter if you scribble down an approximate definition or even draw an arrow from the key part of the phrase to the blank. The point is to save time by getting an idea, even a general one, of what belongs in the blank – not to think of the perfect word (although if you can do that in two seconds, great).

Important: If you can't define with certainty the word that belongs in a blank, do NOT try to plug in something that might only sort of work. That's a great way to set yourself up to overlook the right answer. If you're not sure exactly what belongs in a blank, skip this step and go to step #3.

In addition: for sentences with two blanks, one of the answer choices will contain a common version of a word (e.g. complex), while another will contain a less common synonym (e.g. convoluted). In such cases, you must make sure not to jump right to the simpler version of the word and choose the answer that contains it without plugging in the *other side* to make sure that it fits as well. **On medium and hard questions, the answer choice that contains the more difficult synonym will typically be correct.** For example, consider the following question:

Zoonoses, diseases that jump to humans from animals or to animals from humans, often become more ------- when they are ------- to species that lack immunity.

(A) potent . . susceptible
(B) severe . . attributed
(C) virulent . . transmitted
(D) moderate . . spread
(E) innocuous . . conveyed

Since the sentence is talking about species that *lack* immunity (resistance), you can reasonably assume that that the diseases will become worse. So for your own word, you could try plugging in something like "serious."

Now be careful. When a lot of people look at a sentence like this, they leap right to (B) because "severe" is so obviously a synonym for "serious." The problem is that they *don't* plug in the other side and consider whether it really makes sense. So let's plug it in now:

Zoonoses, diseases that jump to humans from animals or to animals from humans, often become more **severe** when they are **attributed** to species that lack immunity.

What does "attribute" mean? It means "recognize something as the result of a someone's work" (e.g. "The play was **attributed** to Shakespeare"). A disease, however, cannot be "attributed" to a species that's unable to resist it. The sentence is talking about diseases that *jump* from one species to another, so the correct word in the second blank has to be a synonym for "jump." Besides, attributing a disease to a species would not make that disease more serious – there's no relationship between the two things. So (B) does not work.

If you were to work the other way around, you could plug in "jump" for the second blank. Since the word is already defined in the sentence, you don't need to spend time thinking up a word on your own. But here you can run into the same problem. The simplest synonym for "jump" is "spread," which might tempt you to jump to pick (D), but careful! Now the first blank doesn't work. We already know that the first blank has to mean something like "serious," but "moderate" is just the opposite. So it turns out that (D) doesn't work either. (In case you're wondering, the answer is (C) – virulent means "destructive," and "transmitted" fits as a synonym for "spread.")

3) Play positive/negative

If you can't think up your own word, or don't want to waste time trying, use the clues in the sentence determine whether the word(s) in question are positive or negative. It won't always be clear, but when it is, this is an incredibly effective strategy.

If one of the blanks is positive, draw a (+); if it's negative, draw a (–). Do <u>not</u> try to rely on your memory.

Working this way simplifies the process and makes it much more mechanical. It stops you from getting tangled up in nuances and connotations, and from trying to interpret the sentence or read too far into what each answer could make the sentence mean. You don't want to worry about the details until you've eliminated everything that you can eliminate easily.

4) Start eliminating

If you know that one blank is negative, for example, go through each answer from (A) to (E) looking *only* at the second blank. Do not skip around. Going in order keeps you thinking logically and systematically, and reduces the chances that you'll overlook something important.

If the answer fits, keep it; if not, cross out the **entire** answer. Don't just cross out the letter – draw a line through the whole thing. If it's half-wrong, it's wrong.

If you're unsure of whether an answer fits, keep it.

5) Repeat for the other blank

By now you should have gotten rid of at least two answers, sometimes three answers, and if you're really lucky, four answers. Plug the remaining options in and see which works best.

When to Guess and When to Skip

If you are left with more than one answer and are truly unsure of how to determine which one is correct, you should plan to skip the question. Wild guessing will not usually work in your favor, even if you've already eliminated several choices.

If, on the other hand, you can make an educated guess by using a root word (see p. 13 for a discussion of roots and p. 19 for a list of common SAT roots) or by relating a word you are uncertain of to a word you already know, you should answer it. For example, if you don't know what *alleviate* means but can relate it to the painkiller Aleve™, you can make a very good guess about its meaning. In fact, *alleviate* does mean "to lessen pain" or "make better."

As a general rule, any logical process you use to figure out an answer will be at least somewhat effective because it is precisely your ability to reason logically that the SAT is testing. You may not always get the answer for sure, but you'll usually get close enough to make a reasonably confident assumption.

Important: worry about what a word means, not how it sounds.

While some words can clearly be eliminated immediately because they sound thoroughly incorrect in context, you need to consider things much more closely once you get down to a couple of answers.

At that point, you need to ignore the fact that a particular word, one whose meaning is consistent with what the sentence requires, may sound odd or unusual to you. Whether you yourself would think to use a given word is irrelevant – you are simply responsible for identifying the word with the most appropriate meaning. The right answer will not always be the answer you're expecting it to be or the answer you'd like it to be, and you need to realize that you may not be sufficiently well-read to always judge whether a word is truly strange in a particular context.

Using Context Clues to Predict Meanings

Whenever you read a sentence, one of the first things you should look for is the presence of **transition words:** words that indicate logical relationships between parts of the sentence.

Transitions fall into three basic categories:

Continuers

Continuers are words that indicate an idea is continuing in the direction it began.

Key words: and, also, in addition, as well as, furthermore, moreover, similarly, like(wise), even, not only…but also, just as

When they appear, you need to look for **synonyms** for other key words in the sentence, or for words that are generally consistent with those key words. For example:

One of the ------- types of grain, sorghum can withstand harsh
conditions and is especially important in regions where soil is poor
and resources are -------.

Let's just focus on the second blank. The fact that the continuer "and" links the blank to the phrase "soil is poor" tells us that the word we're looking for goes along with the idea of poor soil and must be a negative.

Continuers also include **cause, effect,** and **explanation** words, which indicate that something is causing a particular result or explain why something is occurring.

Key words: so, because, in that, therefore, consequently, as a result

Punctuation: colons, dashes, semicolons (sometimes)

The presence of one of these words or punctuation marks also indicates that you are looking for a word that is **similar** to other key words in the sentence.

For example:

> The first astronauts were required to undergo <u>mental</u> evaluation
> before their flight **because** the ------- danger inherent in space
> travel was judged to be as important as the physiological one.

The transition "because" indicates that the word in the blank must be related to the idea of "mental evaluation" – it must mean something like "psychological."

Contradictors

Contradictors are words that indicate that a sentence is shifting directions, or that contrasting information is being introduced.

> **Key words:** but, however, while, whereas, despite/in spite of, nevertheless, for all (= in spite of), in contrast, unlike, belies

When these words appear, you need to look for **antonyms** for other key words in the sentence, or for words that **contrast** with other key words in the sentence. For example:

> **Although** the southern part of Tunisia is covered by the <u>Sahara desert,</u>
> the remaining areas of the country contain exceptionally ------- soil and
> hundreds of miles of coastline.

The word "although" tells us that the two parts of the sentence contain opposite ideas, and "Sahara desert" tells us that the word in the blank must mean the opposite of "dry" or "barren" – something along the lines of "healthy" or "good."

Parallel Structure

Parallel structure is an idea that you may be familiar with from studying for the multiple-choice Writing section, but it also applies to sentences completions. In such cases, the structure of the sentence itself tells you what sorts of words belong in the blanks. For example:

> The new translation is both -------- and -------: it captures the clarity of the
> original without sacrificing any of its subtlety or complexity.

Alternately, the sentence could be phrased in this way:

> Because it captures the clarity of the original without sacrificing any of its
> subtlety or complexity, the new translation has been praised for its --------
> as well as its --------.

In both cases, the two blanks are intended to run parallel to the two ideas expressed in the sentence. Blank 1 = clarity, Blank 2 = subtlety and complexity.

The colon in the first version and the word "because" in the second indicate the words in the blanks explain or elaborate on the idea that the translation is both subtle and complex.

Important: Two key phrases that sometimes confuse test-takers are *for all*, which means "despite," and *all but*, which means "essentially" or "more or less." These appear frequently, and if you don't know what they mean, it's very easy to misinterpret an entire sentence.

Let's work through a full question now and see how all the pieces fit together:

> Some butterfly species are regarded as **pests** <u>because</u> in
> their larval stages they can ------- crops or trees; <u>however,</u>
> other species play a more ------- role because their cater-
> pillars consume harmful insects.
>
> (A) infect . . detrimental
> (B) destroy . . nefarious
> (C) ruin . . dangerous
> (D) damage . . beneficial
> (E) fertilize . . helpful

The words "pest" and "because" tell us that the word that belongs in the first blank is negative and means something like "harm."

The word "however" indicates that the meaning of the word in the second blank will be the opposite of the meaning of the word in the first blank and will mean something like "nice."

In this case, both blanks are fairly straightforward, so it doesn't really matter which one we start with.

Let's start with the first one. We know it has to be negative, which means we can **eliminate** answers that contain **positive** or **neutral** words. Unfortunately, *infect, destroy, ruin,* and *damage* all fit. Only (E), *fertilize,* is positive. We're going to put a line through the entire answer. Out of sight, out of mind.

> (A) infect . . detrimental
> (B) destroy . . nefarious
> (C) ruin . . dangerous
> (D) damage . . beneficial
> (E) fertilize . . helpful

Now we look at the second blank. We're looking for something positive:

-(A) Detrimental? Negative.

-(B) Nefarious? Maybe you're not sure. Leave it.

-(C) Dangerous? Negative.

-(D) Beneficial? Positive. Definitely works.

So now we're left with this:

~~(A) infect . . detrimental~~
(B) destroy . . nefarious
~~(C) ruin . . dangerous~~
(D) damage . . beneficial
~~(E) fertilize . . helpful~~

Both words clearly work for the first blank; the problem is the second blank.

This is a very common situation: often you can easily get rid of three answers but will be left with two answers choices. You'll know both words for one of the choices, but for the other choice will know only one. Even if you do know what "nefarious" means and can answer this question easily, please bear with me here because this is important.

The rule is that you always work from what you **do** know to what you **don't** know.

If the choice with the words you do know really works – which means that you don't have to "twist" the words at all or understand them in an unusual way to make them fit – then it's the answer. If that choice doesn't work, it's not the answer, and you need to go with the other option.

In this case, *damage . . beneficial* works, so it's the answer. The fact that you might not know what *nefarious* means is irrelevant.

And one more:

> Maria Elena Fernandez is considered an ------- in her field <u>because</u> <u>unlike nearly all present-day journalists</u>, she has a prose style that readers find <u>highly distinctive, even</u> -------.

(A) anomaly . . unmistakable
(B) iconoclast . . redundant
(C) anachronism . . insipid
(D) equivocator . . unforgettable
(E) autocrat . . flippant

The first thing to notice about this sentence is there is no information about the first blank at the beginning of the sentence; its meaning does not become clear until later. So we start with the second blank.

The word "even" tells us that we're looking for a word that is a more extreme form of "distinctive." It's also a positive word because in American culture, standing out or doing something unusual is considered a good thing. I mention this because some of my students who came from cultures that placed a stronger emphasis on conformity have been inclined to view such words negatively.

Going in order, we can eliminate (B), (C), and (E) entirely because *redundant* (repetitive), *insipid* (boring and unoriginal) and *flippant* (not taking something seriously) do not go along with the idea of "distinctive." (A) and (D) both fit.

(A) anomaly . . unmistakable
(B) ~~iconoclast . . redundant~~
(C) ~~anachronism . . insipid~~
(D) equivocator . . unforgettable
(E) ~~autocrat . . flippant~~

At this point, we need to consider the relationship of the first blank to the rest of the sentence, which tells us that Fernandez is *unlike* nearly all other present day journalists – in other words, she's unusual. So which one means unusual, *anomaly* or *equivocator*? Well, keep reading.

Using Roots to Make Educated Guesses

As we've just seen, a familiarity with roots will allow you to make educated guesses about the meanings of words and to quickly identify answers likely to be correct. In fact, learning how to take words apart in order to make reasonable assumptions about their meanings is just as important as memorizing lots of vocabulary words.

In some ways, it is actually far *more* important: if you've simply memorized a lot of definitions, you'll have no way of figuring out whether an unfamiliar word works or not and will be much less certain about the answer you choose. Knowing how the components of a word can reveal its meaning, however, gives you much more flexibility as well as more control, which in turn can give you a lot more confidence.

One of the most important things to remember about the SAT is that it's set up so that you can figure things out. That's what makes it a test of verbal reasoning rather than just an English test. If you have a little background knowledge and think calmly and logically about what's being asked, you can usually come to a reasonable conclusion. It doesn't matter if you're 100% percent sure – that's not the point.

So if you haven't been paying attention in foreign-language class, you might want to start (although admittedly it won't make much of a difference if you study Mandarin). An enormous number of high-frequency words on the SAT have Latin roots, which means that even though the English words being tested may be somewhat esoteric, they are in fact very similar to some extremely *common* French and Spanish and Italian words (everyday words in English tend to have Germanic, or Anglo-Saxon, roots).

If someone uses the word *facile* in English, they'll probably raise some eyebrows. But *facile* means *easy* in French – it's a word that gets used all the time. And if you know what *facile* means, you can make a pretty good assumption about *facility* ("ease"). Likewise, most people don't go around saying *arboreal* in English, but if you know that *arbre, arbòl,* or *albero* means *tree*, you can probably figure it out without too much trouble.

Let's come back to our question from the previous section:

> Maria Elena Fernandez is considered an ------- in her field <u>because</u>
> <u>unlike nearly all present-day journalists</u>, she has a prose style that
> readers find <u>highly distinctive, even</u> -------.
>
> (A) anomaly . . unmistakable
> (B) iconoclast . . redundant
> (C) anachronism . . insipid
> (D) equivocator . . unforgettable
> (E) autocrat . . flippant

Since both *unmistakable* and *unforgettable* fit, we need to decide between *anomaly* and *equivocator*. The root *equi-* means *equal* or *same*, which is the opposite of unusual, so we can make an educated guess that (D) won't work. On the flipside, the prefix *a-* means "not," and we're looking for something that means *not usual*. And in fact the answer is (A). An *anomaly* is something that's highly unusual (*a* = not + *nom* = name → without a name. It doesn't fit exactly, but it's in the same general area).

Let's look at one more example:

> Because he has authored numerous books that draw upon a
> wide range of fields, including many that he has never
> formally studied, Jared Diamond has earned a reputation
> as -------.
>
> (A) a heretic
> (B) a pedant
> (C) a polymath
> (D) an iconoclast
> (E) a pioneer

It's relatively easy to figure out that the word in the blank goes along with the idea of doing a lot of different things: Diamond has written books in a "*wide* range of fields," including "*many* that he has never formally studied." The problem is that when most test-takers look at a set of answers like the one above, they don't recognize any of the words except "pioneer" and maybe "heretic," and then they panic.

In reality, however, the question is much easier than it looks (something that the SAT specializes in) – if you can recognize that the prefix *poly-* means "many." It doesn't matter whether you know the exact definition of "polymath," or even the definitions of the other words. If you know that *poly-* means "many," you can make a very educated guess that (C) is correct (it is).

But, you say, that's only one part of one word. Aren't there a lot of other words there, and couldn't they be important too? In principle, yes; in reality, probably not. The fact that an answer is there doesn't mean it's necessarily relevant. It could just be a plausible-sounding placeholder. Your job is to focus on the information that the question tells you is important and to ignore everything else. If a root in an answer choice is consistent with a key word in the sentence, you need to pay attention.

You can also use roots to figure out whether words are positive or negative – even if you're not certain of the word itself. Sometimes that's the only information you need. Remember this question?

> Some butterfly species are regarded as **pests** <u>because</u> in
> their larval stages they can ------- crops or trees; <u>however,</u>
> other species play a more ------- role because their cater-
> pillars consume harmful insects.
>
> (A) ~~infect . . detrimental~~
> (B) destroy . . nefarious
> (C) ~~ruin . . dangerous~~
> (D) damage . . beneficial
> (E) ~~fertilize . . helpful~~

Let's say for a moment that you weren't sure what *beneficial* meant. In that case, you could use the root *bene-*, which means "good" and always signals a positive word, to help you determine that the answer would fit. Even if you didn't know the definition of *nefarious*, you could still make an educated guess that (D) was the correct answer. To confirm your hunch, you could also observe that *nefarious* starts with *ne-*, like *negative*, and is therefore most likely wrong. And in fact, *nefarious* does mean "cruel."

Roots Can Also Mislead You

While roots can generally help you figure out the meanings of unfamiliar words, they can occasionally be deceptive, too. Words with negative roots can sometimes be positive, and vice-versa. For example:

> Though ------- and even attractive in appearance, nightshade
> has long been recognized as one of the most poisonous plants
> grown in the western hemisphere.
>
> (A) stoic
> (B) innocuous
> (C) toxic
> (D) disquieting
> (E) ephemeral

The phrase "and even attractive in appearance," tells us that the word we're looking for must be positive. "Toxic" is pretty obviously wrong, but after that you might be a little bit stuck.

Here's where playing roots can get you into trouble: if you just go by the fact that *-in* and *-dis* are negative, you'll end up crossing out the right answer. Although words that begin with those prefixes *are* generally negative, in this case, "innocuous" is actually negating a negative: *in* = not + *noc* (Latin *nocere*) = harm → **not** harmful, which is positive and makes perfect sense in the sentence (it is in fact the answer). But to put that together, you have to know two roots – and chances are anyone who knows those roots probably already knows what "innocuous" means as well. Unfortunately, aside from actually knowing what the words mean, there's no guaranteed strategy for recognizing these exceptions – you simply need to be aware that they exist. In general, though, your best bet is to simply use the rules you know: the exceptions are few, and using roots *will* get you the correct answer the vast majority of the time. Worrying about the exceptions can hurt you a lot more than it can help.

Using Relationships to Determine Meanings

Sometimes, a sentence will give you no direct information about the meanings of the words in the blanks. In such cases, however, it will often give you information about the relationship between the words (same/opposite meanings, one a result of the other).

You therefore start by determining that relationship. Is one word the result of the other (both positive or both negative), for example, or is there a transition such as "but" that indicates the words have opposite meanings (one positive, one negative)?

Go through the answer choices looking only at that relationship: if it fits, keep it; if not, cross it out. If you can get down to two or three answers, plug them in and check them in the context of the sentence.

Here again, using roots can be a very effective way of determining relationship if you're not certain of the meanings of the words themselves. You will not be able to apply this strategy to every question, but when you are able to do so, it can be very effective.

For example:

> <u>Far from</u> being -------, the patterns woven into kente cloth, the
> traditional fabric of the Asante people, are created with a great
> deal of -------, with each symbolizing a key value such as family
> unity and collective responsibility.
>
> (A) dogmatic . . wariness
> (B) irrelevant . . candor
> (C) haphazard . . deliberation
> (D) trite . . banality
> (E) esoteric . . efficiency

Since there's no information in the sentence itself that tell us directly what we're looking for, we need to ignore it and just consider the relationship between the words in each choice. (Although if you happen know that kente cloth comes from Africa and that the SAT is generally positive toward all things African and African-American, you *can* make an educated guess that the second blank is positive and that the first blank is negative.)

Notice that most of the answer choices are "hard" words – this question tests both your ability to follow the logic of the sentence and your knowledge of the words themselves.

(A) dogmatic = holding rigidly to a belief; wariness = suspicious. Yes, opposites.

(B) irrelevant = not relevant; candor = openness, directness. No relationship.

(C) haphazard = by chance; deliberation = on purpose, with great care. Yes, opposites.

(D) trite and banality = unoriginal. No, same.

(E) esoteric = beyond normal understanding; efficiency = without waste. No relationship.

Now we're down to (A) and (C). *Dogmatic* is really only used to talk about a person's adherence to a belief or idea. And *wariness*? There's nothing in the sentence to explain why someone would be suspicious of cloth.

So the answer is (C). Logically, it makes sense that cloth-makers would use great care in choosing patterns that symbolize *key values*.

If you had no idea whether the words in (C) were opposites, though, and had been paying close attention in French class, you could figure it out this way: you probably know that *deliberately* means "on purpose," so the question is *haphazard*. *Hap-* is like "happen," and in French, *hasard* means chance, hence *haphazard* means "happens by chance."

Will figuring out the answer that way be a big stretch for most people? Yes, of course. But that's beside the point. The point is that there is an underlying logic to the answer choices, and you can use that logic to help you figure things out. If you approach studying for sentence completions with that idea in mind, you'll already be ahead.

Second Meanings are Usually Right

One of the cardinal rules of SAT sentence completions is that the closer you get to the end of the section, the less you can take for granted. On #1 or 2, or even #3, you can be pretty sure that if a word doesn't initially appear to fit the sentence, it's not going to be the answer. The same does not hold true at the end of the section, however. Mindlessly eliminating words that seem obviously – perhaps too obviously – wrong can get you in a good deal of trouble.

Sometimes the word that you want to show up just won't be among the answer choices, and sometimes the right answer is something that never would have occurred to you – even if you'd spent ten minutes staring at the question. That's why #8 is #8 and not #2. And that's also why, as you get close to the end of a section, you need to be particularly on the lookout for words that are being used in their second or third meaning. Why? Because the people at ETS know that those are the last words that it would occur to most test-takers to pick – which is precisely why they're likely to be correct. (Those psychometricians at the College Board may be nasty, but after hearing dozens of students say, "I never ever would have thought to pick that," I have to admit that they're remarkably accurate.)

But here we have a problem: it's not much help to know that second meanings are usually right if you can't recognize them! Admittedly, there's no surefire way around it. **As a general rule of thumb, though, you need to pay particular attention to "easy" words on hard questions, especially on the last question of a section, where second meanings are most likely to appear**. If you're on question #8 and see a simple word that seems too obviously wrong, you might need to think again. There's a pretty good chance it's being used in some other way. And if it's being used in some other way, there's a good chance it's correct.

For example:

> Because the Symbolists believed that art should ------- absolute
> truths that can only be described indirectly, they wrote in a highly
> metaphorical and ------- manner.
>
> (A) suggest . . garrulous
> (B) convey . . lucid
> (C) represent . . elliptical
> (D) resist . . fervent
> (E) insist on . . cantankerous

Since the sentence provides relatively little information about the first blank, the key to the question is the second phrase. The word "and" tells us that the meaning of the second blank is a general synonym for "highly metaphorical." Scanning just the second side, a lot of people would, however, immediately jump to cross out *elliptical* because they associate ellipses with math or physics class and assume that they couldn't possibly have anything to do with art. The problem is that *elliptical* can also mean *obscure*, *cryptic*, or *impenetrable* – synonyms for "highly metaphorical." So in fact it fits perfectly; the answer is (C).

Common Roots and Prefixes

Positive

Ama - Love
amiable = easy to get along with

Amic - Friend
amicable = friendly

Ana - Not, without
Anarchy = without rule

Bene - Good
beneficial = helpful, good
(bene + fic = do, something that does good)

Eu - Happy
Euphoria = joyful exhilaration
Euphonic = pleasant sounding

Fid - Loyal
perfidy = disloyal
(per = through or beyond+ fid = literally "beyond loyalty")

Lev - Light (weight)
alleviate = to relieve from pain, literally "to make lighter"

Luc, Lux - Light (absence of dark)
lucid = clear

Magna - Large
magnanimous = very generous
(magna + anim, soul/spirit = greatness of spirit)

Moll - Soft
emollient = substance that softens
mollify = pacify, calm down, literally "make soft"

Multi - Many
multifarious = complex, having many different aspects

Pac, Plac - Peace
placate = to soothe, make peaceful

Poly - Many
polymath = person knowledgeable about or accomplished in many different areas

Pro - In favor of
prolong = make longer

Val - Value
Valid = True, literally "having value"

Vener - Worship, Love
venerate = hold in high regard

Ver - True
verisimilitude = appearance of truth
(ver + simil, similar = similar to the truth)

Vig - Energy
vigorous = energetic, full of life

Negative

A - Not, Without
anomalous = unusual, lit. "without name"

Anti - Against
antipathy = dislike

Bell - War
belligerent, bellicose = threatening, violent

Contra - Against
contrast = difference

Culp - Guilt
exculpate = free from guilt

Deb - Weak
debilitate = to make weak, cripple

Dis - Not
disparage = to put down, insult

Err - Wrong
erroneous = wrong

Fall - Wrong
fallacious = false

Fict - False
fictitious = fake, false

Im, In - Not
ineffable = inexpressible

Pej - Bad
pejorative = insulting

Pug - Violent
pugnacious = violent, looking for a fight

Vac - Empty OR Waver
vacuous = empty, meaningless

Neutral or positive/negative based on context

Ambi - Both
ambivalent = having mixed feelings, unable to choose between two sides

Ante - Before
antebellum = before the war
(ante + bellum, war)

Anthro - Human
Misanthrope = one who hates people

Auto - Self
autonomous = independent

Bi - Two
Bifurcate = split down the middle

Chron - Time
anachronism = in the wrong time period (a record player is an anachronism in the 21st century)
(ana = not + chron = not in time)

Circum - Around
circumspect = careful, cautious
(circum + spect, look = to look around)

Co, Con - With
condescending = looking down on, disdainful

Cog - Think
cognition = thought

Corp - Body
corporeal = having a body

Di - Two
dichotomy = contradictory, separated into two mutually exclusive groups or ideas

Dia - Through
dialect = regional or local form of a language
(dia + lect, read = read through)

Dict - Say
dictum = saying, cliché

Dom - Mastery
dominate = have power over

Dur - Hard, Lasting
endure = last

E, Ex - From
extemporaneous = done without
preparation
(ex + temp, time = away from time)

Equi - Equal, Same
equivocal = unclear or using ambiguous
language, sometimes with the intention to
mislead (equi + voc, voice = literally
"equal voice")

Fac, Fic - Make, do
facile = easy (literally "doable")

Gen - Knowledge, Innate, Type
ingenuous = naive
(in = not + gen = not having knowledge)
genetic = from the genes, innate

Grav - Weight, Serious
gravity = seriousness

Hetero - Different
heterogeneous = varied, multifaceted
(hetero + gen = different types)

Homo - Same
homogeneous = same
(homo + gen = same type)

Inter - Between
interrupt = come between

Lib - Free OR Book
liberate = to set free

Loc, Loq - Words, Speech
loquacious = talkative

Mal - Bad
malicious = cruel, evil

Ment - Mind
mentality = mindset

Morph - Shape
amorphous = shapeless

Mut - Change
immutable = fixed, unchanging
(im = not + mut)

Nerv - boldness, courage
enervate – to sap of energy
(e = from + nerv = take away courage)

Nom - Name
nominal = literally "in name only"

Ob - Against
obdurate, obstinate = extremely stubborn

Os - Bone
ossify = become hard, like bone

Para - Alongside, Contrary to
Paradox = contradiction, two seemingly
contradictory ideas

Ped - Child
pedestrian = boring, unoriginal (literally,
"like a child would do")

Pend - Hang
pendulous = hanging, heavy

Per - Through
perspicacious = perceptive
(per + spic = look, look through)

Peri - Around
periphery = border

Phon - Sound
euphony = pleasing sounds
(eu, happy + phon)

Port - Carry
portentous = significant, amazing (literally "carrying a lot of weight")

Pot - Power
potent = powerful, potentate = a powerful person

Re - Again
revive = bring back to life
(re + viv, live = make live again)

Scrut - Look, Examine
Scrutinize = look very closely

Sens, Sent - Feel
sentimental = emotional, displaying or appealing to tender feelings

Seq - Follow
obsequious = follower, toady

Spec/Spect - Look
spectator = one who watches

Stat - Stand
static = unmoving, literally "in a state of standing"

Sub - Below
substantiate = support, prove (literally "stand below")

Super - Above
supercilious = condescending (looking down on)

Tac - Silence
taciturn = silent, not talkative

Temp - Time
temporize = procrastinate, take too much time

Ten - Hold
tenacious = stubborn, "holding on"

Terr - Earth
Terrestrial = having to do with the earth

Tract - Move
intractable = stubborn

Trans - Through
intransigent = stubborn, unmovable

Vap - Air, Steam
evaporate = to become air

Ven - Come
advent = beginning, literally "coming of"

Vid, Vis - See
invisible = unable to be seen

Vit, Viv - Life
convivial = merry, lively
(con = with + viv = with life)

Voc, Vox - Voice
vociferous = loud

Vol - Desire, Fly (v.), Volume
volatile = unstable, having the potential to explode (literally "ready to fly off")

Volut - Turn, Twist
convoluted = extremely intricate/complex
(con = with + volut = turn, literally "with lots of turns")

Vocabulary Lists

List 1

Adroit
Capricious
Circumspect
Didactic
(Un)equivocal/equivocate
Esoteric
Ineffable
Magnanimous
Obsequious
Pedantic
Pedestrian
Pragmatic
Quixotic
Sycophant
Tacit(urn)

List 2

Aloof
Banal
Censure
(Dis)ingenuous
Disparage
Duplicitous
Eschew
Extol
Heterogeneous
Iconoclast
Innocuous
Laconic
Meticulous
Mitigate
Substantiate/
unsubstantiated

List 3

Alleviate
Assiduous

Bellicose
Convoluted
Cosmopolitan
Deleterious
Ephemeral
Obstinate
Paradigm
Scrutinize/inscrutable
Superfluous
Transitory
Undermine
Venerate
Wary

List 4

Abstruse
Ascetic
Bombastic
Candid
Contemptuous
Derivative
Gregarious
Hackneyed
Motley
Penchant
Provincial
Supercilious
Tout
Vitriolic
Whimsical

List 5

Acquiesce
Acumen
Aesthetic
Assuage
Benign

Bucolic
Caustic
Diligent
Eclectic
Flippant
Hackneyed
(In)tractable
Laud
Munificent
Trite

List 6

Anomaly
Capitulate
Charlatan
Heretic
Immutable
Insipid
Intrepid
Lucid
Mundane
Obdurate
Partisan
Penury
Surreptitious
Tenacious
Vindicate

List 7

Adept
Alacrity
Diffident
Disseminate
Enigmatic
Exonerate
Loquacious
Mirthful
Parsimonious
Prosaic

Reticent
Soporific
Succinct
Tangential
Vapid
Zealot

List 8

Abate
Belligerent
Cacophony
Circumscribe
Dilettante
Euphemism
Garrulous
Jovial
Misanthrope
Parochial
Perfidy
Protean
Pugnacious
Vacuous
Venerate

List 9

Byzantine
Chary
Dearth
Dogmatic
Exculpate
Expedient
Fervid/fervent
Forestall
Harbinger
Interminable
Myriad
Obtuse
Paragon
Prolific
Serendipity

List 10

Amiable/amicable
Coerce/coercion
Condone
Contentious
Disparage
Dormant
Idiosyncratic
Infallible
Mundane
Myriad
Peripheral
Placate
Recondite
Revere
Zenith

List 11

Amorphous
Arbitrary
Benevolent
Elated
Enthrall
Impugn
Ludicrous
Marginal
Paucity
Perfunctory
Polemical
Sanguine
Sardonic
Terse
Vacillate

List 12

Aplomb
Augment
Cantankerous
Disdain
Epitome
Foible

Haphazard
Indignant
Mellifluous
Obstreperous
Predilection
Redolent
Renounce
Sanction
Stoic

List 13

Abeyance
Astute
Castigate
Circumvent
Congenial
Diatribe
Incredulous
Maudlin
Maverick
Prolific
Prurient
Rectitude
Utilitarian
Veracity

List 14

Adversary
Anachronistic
Cavalier
Dispel
Indelible
Jingoistic
Mercurial
Palliate
Perspicacious
Platitude
Profligacy
Quotidian
Stipulate
Vindicate
Voracious

List 15

Admonish
Amalgam
Ambivalent
Arduous
Buoyant
Captious
Copious
Dichotomy
Evade
Lackadaisical
Permutation
Propensity
Pundit
Quibble
Subvert

List 16

Ancillary
Belabor
Callous
Dilatory
Fortuitous
Germane
Ingenious
Intransigent
Mendacious
Obstreperous
Prescient
Recalcitrant
Stipulate
Vestige
Wistful

List 17

Austere
Bemused
Candid
Conciliatory
Deride
Dilettante

Erudite
Hapless
Indigent
Nonplussed
Onerous
Parochial
Renege
Spurious
Stilted

List 18

Averse/aversion
Baleful
Chicanery
Compunction
Discrete
Elated
Fallacious
Forestall
Indigenous
Itinerant
Paragon
Rancor
Repudiate
Specious
Trenchant

List 19

Appease
Bolster
Cajole
Expostulate
Fleeting
Implacable
Impromptu
Mercenary
Officious
Ostentatious
Peripatetic
Philanthropist
Preclude
Unprecedented

Volatile

List 20

Adulation
Conjecture
Cursory
Expurgate
Exultant
Florid
Malleable
Mimetic
Multifarious
Nominal
Portentous
Propitiatory
Sybaritic
Tenacious
Vituperate
Voluble

List 21

Eulogy
Euphony
Excavate
Exhort
Dispassionate
Facetious
Fortuitous
Germane
Mawkish
Nadir
Ostensible
Panache
Plasticity
Proclivity
Demur

List 22

Denizen
Divulge
Expedite

Extemporaneous
Imperious
Judicious
Libel
Myopic
Polymath
Rapacious
Ruminate
Sheepish
Sophistry
Torpid/Torpor
Voluptuous

List 23

Acrimony
Apprise
Bashful
Beguile
Conflate
Delectable
Edify
Empiricism
Explicate
Fickle
Inculcate
Rebut
Reiterate
Resuscitate

List 24

Blunder
Connoisseur
Equanimity
Forbearance
Imperturbable
Meld
Nullify
Ratify
Reconcile
Rectitude
Rhetoric
Solvent

Synthesize
Truncate
Watershed

List 25

Aspersion
Becalm
Denigrate
Denounce
Disquiet
Flustered
Humbuggery
Indispensable
Picayune
Platitude/Platitudinous
Protégé
Quackery
Redundant
Serene
Unwieldy

Top Words By Category

Positive	Negative
Smart and Original	**Boring and Unoriginal**
Adroit	Banal
Astute	Clichéd
Adept	Derivative
Acumen ("knowhow")	Hackneyed
Ingenious	Mundane
Innovative	Pedestrian
Perspicacious	Prosaic
Sagacious	Quotidian
	Trite
	Vacuous
Friendly/Easygoing	Vapid
Ami(c)able	**Stubborn**
Congenial	
Docile	Intractable
Tractable	Intransigent
	Obdurate
	Obstinate
Give into	Recalcitrant
	Tenacious
Acquiesce	Timid/timorous
Capitulate	
Indulge	**Quiet/Shy**
Outgoing/Talkative	Aloof
	Diffident
Garrulous	Laconic
Gregarious	Tacit(urn)
Loquacious	
Voluble	**Angry/Violent**
Happy	Bellicose
	Belligerent
Ebullient	Caustic
Elated	Intemperate
Exultant	Irascible
Jovial	Pugnacious
Mirthful	Vitriolic
Sanguine	
	Destroy
Have a Liking For	
	Eradicate
Bent	Extirpate
Penchant	Obliterate
Predilection	
Proclivity	

Positive	Negative
Praise and Admiration	**Criticism and Punishment**
Acclaim	Abhor
Accolades	Admonish
Adulate	Censure
Extol	Chastise
Laud	Deride
Plaudits	Disdain
Revere	Disparage
Tout	Excoriate
Venerate	Loathe
	Malign
	Rebuke
	Revile
	Vituperate
To Lessen (Pain)/Soothe	**Make Worse**
Alleviate	Aggravate
Ameliorate	Exacerbate
Assuage	
Mitigate	
Palliate	
Hardworking/Detail-Oriented	**Lazy and Careless**
Assiduous	Apathetic
Diligent	Haphazard
Meticulous	Indifferent
Punctilious	Indolent
Sedulous	Lackadaisical
	Poor
Generous	Impecunious
	Indigent
Alruist(ic)	Penurious
Magnanimous	
Munificent	
Philanthropy/Philanthropic	**Impractical**
Practical	Idealistic
	Quixotic
Pragmatic	
Prudent	

Positive	Negative
Large Amount	**Small Amount**
Comprehensive	Circumscribed
Copious	Dearth
Myriad	Paucity
Plethora	
Diverse	**Narrow-Minded**
Eclectic	Insular
Heterogeneous	Parochial
Motley	Provincial
Multifarious	
Sophisticated	**Naïve and Idealistic**
Cosmopolitan	Callow
	Ingenuous
	Quixotic
Deep Knowledge	**Dry and Boring**
Arcane	Pedantic
Erudite	Soporific
Esoteric	
Profound/profundity	
Recondite	
Clear and Direct	**Unclearness and Indecision**
Candid	Equivocal/equivocate
Economical	Nebulous
Lucid	Obfuscate
Perspicuous	Vacillate
Succinct	Waver
Terse	
Unequivocal	**Complicated**
	Byzantine
	Convoluted
Calm	**Nervous**
Phlegmatic	
Serene	Apprehensive
Unflappable	Flustered
Unruffled	Nonplussed

Positive	Negative
Unpredictable/Playful	**Lying and Fraudulence**
Capricious	Charlatan
Droll	Chicanery
Impetuous	Mendacious
Mercurial	Prevaricate
Whimsical	Specious
	Spurious
Spread Around, Promote	**Short-Lived**
Disperse	Cursory
Disseminate	Ephemeral
Perpetuate	Fleeting
Propagate	
	Arrogant
Free from Guilt	Condescending
Exculpate	Contemptuous
Exonerate	Disdain(ful)
Penitent	Supercilious
Repent	
	Unimportant
Important	Ancillary
Acclaimed	Eschew
Eminent	Inconsequential
	Jettison
Examine Closely	Negligible
	Peripheral
Peruse	Trivial(ize)
Scrutinize	
	Prevent
	Hinder/Hindrance
	Preclude
	Stymie
	Thwart
	Undermine
	Suspicious
	Chary
	Incredulous
	Skeptical
	Wary
	Manipulate
	Cajole
	Coerce

Common Second Meanings

Afford – Grant (e.g. an opportunity)

Appreciate – To take into account, recognize the merits of, OR to increase in value

Arrest – To stop (not just put handcuffs on a criminal)

Assume – To take on responsibility for, acquire (e.g. to assume a new position)

Austerity – Financial policy to reduce excess spending on luxury or non-essential items

Badger – To pester or annoy (e.g. reporters repeatedly badgered the candidate after news of the scandal broke)

Bent – Liking for. Synonym for *penchant, predilection, proclivity*

Capacity – Ability

Chance – To attempt

Check – To restrain, control, or reduce (e.g. *The vaccine checked the spread of the disease*)

Coin – Invent (e.g. coin a phrase)

Compromise – To endanger or make vulnerable (e.g. to compromise one's beliefs)

Constitution – Build (e.g. a football play has a solid constitution)

Consummate – Total, absolute (e.g. a consummate professional)

Conviction – Certainty, determination. Noun form of *convinced*.

Couch – To hide

Curious – Strange

Discriminating – Able to make fine distinctions (e.g. someone who can detect subtle flavors has a *discriminating* palate).

Dispatch – Speed, efficiency (e.g. *She completed the project promptly and with great dispatch*)

Doctor – To tamper with

Economy – Thrift (e.g. a writer who has an *economical* style is one who uses few words)

Embroider – To falsify, make up stories about

Execute – To carry out

Exploit – Make use of (does not carry a negative connotation)

Facility – Ability to do something easily (e.g. *a facility for learning languages*)

Foil – To get in the way of, put a stop to (e.g. to foil a robbery), OR a secondary, often comedic character in a play or novel, used to emphasize the good qualities of the hero.

Grave/Gravity – Serious(ness)

Grill – To question intensely and repeatedly (e.g. *The police officers grilled the suspect thoroughly*)

Hamper – To get in the way of, hinder

Harbor – To possess, hold (e.g. to harbor a belief)

Hobble – Prevent, impede

Mint – To produce money, or as an adjective = perfect, like new

Provoke – Elicit (e.g. a reaction)

Qualify – Provide more information about or a more nuanced understanding of

Realize – To achieve (a goal)

Reconcile – To bring together opposing or contradictory ideas

Relate – To tell, give an account of (a story)

Relay – To pass on to someone else (e.g. to relay information)

Reservations – Misgivings

Reserve – To hold off on (e.g. to reserve judgment)

Ruffled – Flustered, nonplussed

Sap – To drain (e.g. of energy)

Scrap – To eliminate

Shelve/Table – To reject or discard (e.g. an idea or proposal)

Solvent – Able to pay all debts (usually used in a business context)

Sound – Firm, stable, reliable, valid (e.g. a sound argument)

Spare, Severe – Unadorned, very plain

Static – Unchanging (i.e. in a state of *stasis*)

Sustain – To withstand

Uniform – Constant, unvarying

Unqualified – Absolute

Upset – To interfere with an expected outcome

Exercise: Breaking it Down (Answers p. 82)

Directions:

1) Identify and underline or circle the key words or phrase that provide information about the meaning of each blank.

2) Either fill in your own word or indicate whether each blank requires a positive or a negative word by writing a (+) or a (–) in the blank. Note that this strategy will not be applicable to every sentence.

3) For two blanks sentences, consider each side separately, eliminating the **entire answer** when one side does not fit.

4) When you have completed steps 1-3, look at the answer choices provided, select the answer that logically fits the sentence.

1. In Ancient Egyptian art, human figures are presented in a rigid and ------- manner; in contrast, animals are often very well-observed and lifelike.

   Circle or underline key words

   Definition or (+/-): _____

   (A) dazzling
   (B) artificial
   (C) revolutionary
   (D) satirical
   (E) realistic

2. The outwardly ------- appearance of the Afar Triangle, one of the world's most geologically active regions, belies the presence of fiery pools of lava lying just beneath its surface.

   Circle or underline key words

   Definition or (+/-): _____

   (A) placid
   (B) noxious
   (C) cavernous
   (D) belligerent
   (E) ludicrous

3. Though well-done and expressive, Van Gogh's early drawings never succeed in approaching the level of ------- that marks his most celebrated works.

   Circle or underline key words

   Definition or (+/-): _____

   (A) mediocrity
   (B) instability
   (C) virtuosity
   (D) serenity
   (E) efficiency

4. Because female hyenas remain within their clan and inherit their mother's rank, sisters must compete with one another to obtain a ------- position in the hierarchy.

   Circle or underline key words

   Definition or (+/-): _____

   (A) relative
   (B) cumbersome
   (C) dominant
   (D) surreptitious
   (E) peripheral

5. Because music plays an essential role in facilitating social functions, researchers are beginning to question whether it truly is as ------- as they once believed.

Circle or underline key words

Definition or (+/-): _____

(A) aesthetic
(B) mellifluous
(C) demanding
(D) invigorating
(E) frivolous

6. Paradoxically, the attainment of creative success nearly always requires the ------- of a cherished ideal or familiar way of working.

Circle or underline key words

(A) stipulation
(B) renunciation
(C) embellishment
(D) repetition
(E) dissemination

Definition or (+/-): _____

7. The camera obscura was perhaps the earliest known imaging device, --------- of the modern-day photographic camera.

Circle or underline key words

Definition or (+/-): _____

(A) a descendant
(B) a forerunner
(C) a relic
(D) a proponent
(E) an heir

8. To recreate the daily activities of Renaissance merchants as well as their worldview, the exhibition includes paintings and mercantile -------, from weighty ledgers to nautical maps.

Circle or underline key words

Definition or (+/-): _____

(A) diatribes
(B) paraphernalia
(C) caveats
(D) foibles
(E) euphemisms

9. English botanist James Edward Smith demonstrated a ------- interest in science, exhibiting an intense fascination with the natural world from the earliest years of his childhood.

Circle or underline key words

Definition or (+/-): _____

(A) cursory
(B) trivial
(C) hackneyed
(D) precocious
(E) circumspect

10. The company's leaders have a poor record of keeping their promises, suggesting that they will be unable to meet the ------- set out by union officials in the new contract.

Circle or underline key words

Definition or (+/-): _____

(A) innovations
(B) quandaries
(C) stipulations
(D) enigmas
(E) dichotomies

In the following questions, the answer choices for the two blanks have been separated so that you must consider each side separately. Do not mix and match answer choices – if you choose (A) for the first blank, you must also choose (A) for the second blank.

11. For centuries, ------- have questioned the authorship of Shakespeare's plays, ------- no fewer than fifty alternative candidates that include Francis Bacon, Queen Elizabeth I, and Christopher Marlowe.

Circle or underline key words

1st Definition or (+/-): _____

2nd Definition or (+/-): _____

First Blank:

(A) partisans
(B) detractors
(C) skeptics
(D) naysayers
(E) zealots

Second Blank:

(A) rejecting
(B) exonerating
(C) proffering
(D) embellishing
(E) detaining

Remaining Possibilities:

Answer: _____

12. If it is to succeed, any new ------- for resolving disputes between workers and management must include a less ------- review board, one with members who are independent and neutral experts.

Circle or underline key words

1st Definition or (+/-): _____

2nd Definition or (+/-): _____

First Blank:

(A) paradigm
(B) proposal
(C) construct
(D) idea
(E) consensus

Second Blank:

(A) partisan
(B) erudite
(C) adept
(D) disinterested
(E) litigious

Remaining Possibilities:

Answer: _____

13. All of the factors that allowed the Great Barrier Reef to ------- are changing at unprecedented rates and may cause it to ------- below a crucial threshold from which it cannot recover.

Circle or underline key words

1st Definition or (+/-): _____

2nd Definition or (+/-): _____

First Blank:

(A) grow
(B) diminish
(C) exist
(D) thrive
(E) flourish

Second Blank:

(A) evolve
(B) recover
(C) forestall
(D) deteriorate
(E) crest

Remaining Possibilities:

Answer: _____

14. Although traditional historians and historical filmmakers differ in their choice of medium, the most respected ones share a ------- regard for facts and the rules of evidence that ------- their acceptability.

Circle or underline key words

1st Definition or (+/-): _____

2nd Definition or (+/-): _____

First Blank:

(A) blatant
(B) capricious
(C) pedantic
(D) sporadic
(E) scrupulous

Second Blank:

(A) mock
(B) determine
(C) derive
(D) underlie
(E) dictate

Remaining Possibilities:

Answer: _____

Easy (Answers p. 84)

1. One of the most educated women of her era, Queen Elizabeth I was a noted -------: she spoke French, Italian, and Spanish as well as Welsh and Cornish.

    (A) monarchist
    (B) patron
    (C) misanthrope
    (D) polyglot
    (E) sovereign

2. In the decades after moveable type was invented, many booksellers ------- machine-printed books because they considered handmade books to be of higher quality.

    (A) recommended
    (B) disparaged
    (C) embellished
    (D) salvaged
    (E) accumulated

3. While the cheetah's extinction no longer seems imminent, the number of cheetahs living in the wild has ------- from roughly 100,000 in 1900 to barely 10,000 today.

    (A) migrated
    (B) plummeted
    (C) capitulated
    (D) defected
    (E) proliferated

4. Writers in the magical realist tradition often use characters with -------- powers such as levitation, flight, and ESP in order to subtly comment on contemporary social issues.

    (A) fantastical
    (B) nefarious
    (C) creative
    (D) unpredictable
    (E) delusional

5. Philosopher Simone Weil possessed an exceptional sense of -------; for example, she refused to eat sugar after she heard that soldiers fighting in World War I were forced to go without.

    (A) erudition
    (B) objectivity
    (C) empathy
    (D) contempt
    (E) sophistry

6. Fracking, the process of extracting natural gas from shale, has been criticized by ------- for contaminating groundwater and creating methane leaks.

    (A) denizens
    (B) detractors
    (C) benefactors
    (D) acolytes
    (E) solicitors

7. The python has a ------- diet: it consumes bobcats, deer, opossums, and more than twenty-five species of birds.

    (A) salutary
    (B) restricted
    (C) naturalistic
    (D) exclusive
    (E) heterogeneous

8. While there is overwhelming evidence that exercise is ------- to health in most people, new research suggests that too much physical exertion can have ------- effects on the body.

    (A) detrimental . . harmful
    (B) advantageous . . salutary
    (C) dangerous . . perilous
    (D) inimical . . pervasive
    (E) beneficial . . deleterious

9. For nearly a decade, Olympic champion
    Michelle Kwan enjoyed ------- level of
    popularity; no ice-skater had ever received
    such extensive media coverage.

    (A) an inexplicable
    (B) a trivial
    (C) an unprecedented
    (D) an unsustainable
    (E) a recurrent

10. Weather in the Grand Canyon -------
    according to -------: the forested rim is high
    enough to receive snowfall, but in lower
    areas, warm temperatures predominate.

    (A) changes . . climate
    (B) accelerates . . topography
    (C) varies . . wilderness
    (D) stabilizes . . location
    (E) fluctuates . . elevation

11. The ------- of the city's historic quarter has
    prompted both residents and preservationists
    to rally for its restoration.

    (A) urbanity
    (B) decrepitude
    (C) vigor
    (D) compunction
    (E) density

12. The suppression of low-intensity forest fires
    inevitably leads to more dangerous fires
    because ------- materials that would
    otherwise be destroyed are allowed to -------.

    (A) incendiary . . dissipate
    (B) insoluble . . flourish
    (C) terrestrial . . demolish
    (D) combustible . . accumulate
    (E) flammable . . entangle

13. Philadelphia's population soared during the
    nineteenth century because of ------- of
    immigrants from Europe and the southern
    United States.

    (A) an abeyance
    (B) a diminution
    (C) a consensus
    (D) an evacuation
    (E) an influx

14. Charles Mingus's music ------- the listener in
    the blues rituals of African American life,
    while at the same time depicting those rituals
    from a playful distance.

    (A) harmonizes
    (B) identifies
    (C) complements
    (D) immerses
    (E) validates

15. Museum administrators were sharply
    ------- after it was revealed that they had
    authorized the purchase of stolen antiquities.

    (A) mollified
    (B) esteemed
    (C) rebuked
    (D) exasperated
    (E) desecrated

16. In seventeenth-century England, puns
    allowed ordinary people to make light of
    their superiors without directly ------- the
    established social order.

    (A) improving
    (B) constructing
    (C) undermining
    (D) stabilizing
    (E) unifying

SAT Sentence Completion Workbook

17. At the end of World War II, the Allies created a government that would ------- power throughout Germany in order to limit the influence of any single region.

    (A) legislate
    (B) disperse
    (C) justify
    (D) exploit
    (E) demonstrate

18. George Washington Carver is believed to have been born in January of 1864; however, the exact date of his birth remains -------.

    (A) evident
    (B) speculative
    (C) celebratory
    (D) unattainable
    (E) annual

19. Genoa ------- rapidly after its defeat at the battle of Chioggia in 1380, eventually losing its ------- and falling under foreign rule.

    (A) deteriorated . . rivalry
    (B) thrived . . autonomy
    (C) abated . . uniqueness
    (D) improved . . cosmopolitanism
    (E) declined . . independence

20. The source of Mark Twain's (Samuel Langhorne Clemens') pen name has long been a mystery, but new evidence suggests that this -------- may soon be resolved.

    (A) enigma
    (B) dichotomy
    (C) tradition
    (D) aptitude
    (E) fallacy

Medium (Answers p. 88)

1. Simran's teammates are impressed by her -------; she shows no reaction when she is injured or experiences physical discomfort.

    (A) stoicism
    (B) impetuousness
    (C) perspicacity
    (D) munificence
    (E) gregariousness

2. The impact of the poor economy is reflected in the ------- of families able to afford a vacation this year.

    (A) confluence
    (B) dearth
    (C) glut
    (D) deprivation
    (E) spate

3. Hildegard of Bingen was among the most ------- writers and composers of the Middle Ages, producing hundreds of songs, letters, and treatises.

    (A) condescending
    (B) lauded
    (C) magnanimous
    (D) anachronistic
    (E) prolific

4. Pauline Kael is often viewed as ------- because she re-invented film criticism as an art form and pioneered an entirely new style of writing.

    (A) an iconoclast
    (B) a dilettante
    (C) an adversary
    (D) a charlatan
    (E) a jingoist

5. Modern science is based on the notion that scientific truth is simple and --------, devoid of the ------- found in literature.

    (A) lofty . . versatility
    (B) objective . . industriousness
    (C) unequivocal . . ambiguity
    (D) irate . . diversity
    (E) adaptive . . instability

6. Nineteenth century Romantic writers ------- the revision process, insisting that the best literature flowed from spontaneous and ------- creative acts.

    (A) curated . . sophisticated
    (B) detested . . egregious
    (C) excoriated . . militant
    (D) spurned . . organic
    (E) organized . . whimsical

7. Research suggests that the brain is not organized like ------- with a clear chain of command, but is in fact a turbulent ------- of surprisingly independent cells and neurons.

    (A) a regiment . . summary
    (B) a democracy . . environment
    (C) an incentive . . network
    (D) a hierarchy . . amalgam
    (E) an intuition. . panoply

8. Matisse was both ------- and ------- : he belonged to no officially recognized school of artists, and was known for his undeniably odd behavior.

    (A) innovative . . versatile
    (B) aloof . . eccentric
    (C) intense . . unconventional
    (D) rebellious . . ascetic
    (E) whimsical . . peculiar

9. Carbon has an importance that is ------- to its -------: it is the key constituent of precious materials from diamonds to oil but makes up less than 0.1 percent of the Earth's bulk.

    (A) common . . density
    (B) disproportionate . . sparseness
    (C) detrimental . . effectiveness
    (D) exclusive . . utility
    (E) indispensable . . durability

10. In some fictional dystopias, such as that portrayed in Margaret Atwood's novel *The Handmaid's Tale*, the family has been ------- as a social institution, and continuing efforts are made to prevent its -------

    (A) obliterated . . resolution
    (B) constructed . . resurrection
    (C) promoted . . protection
    (D) eradicated . . resurgence
    (E) abolished . . dissolution

11. While Jackson Pollock's early work is in some ways quite -------, it nevertheless hints at some of the more ------- aspects of his emerging artistic personality.

    (A) imaginative . . irreverent
    (B) intriguing . . mercurial
    (C) simplistic . . aesthetic
    (D) perplexing . . confounding
    (E) hackneyed . . innovative

12. As bits and pieces left over from the formation of the solar system, near-Earth objects provide important insights into the environment of the ------- planets.

    (A) celestial
    (B) nascent
    (C) luminous
    (D) imperturbable
    (E) elliptical

13. Although he often lamented his -------, Walter Benjamin was actually quite energetic and productive as a writer.

(A) vivaciousness
(B) benevolence
(C) joviality
(D) indolence
(E) abstemiousness

14. Over the decades, literary sleuths have turned up numerous journalistic sins in Truman Capote's "In Cold Blood," ranging from minor ------- to outright -------.

(A) deficiencies . . reconciliation
(B) inaccuracies . . fabrication
(C) revelations . . abstraction
(D) platitudes . . indiscretion
(E) lapses . . classification

15. When asked to predict the outcome of the election, the journalist -------, alternately predicting that the current front-runner and a more obscure candidate would prevail.

(A) vacillated
(B) desisted
(C) theorized
(D) dissented
(E) capitulated

16. The city's financial struggles are particularly ------- because they did not result from a single event but rather developed from ------- of factors.

(A) crippling . . a paucity
(B) grave . . a diminution
(C) acute . . an invocation
(D) benign . . a deluge
(E) dire . . a confluence

17. Although the book has been well-received and has even won several awards, the ------ of its scope does occasionally ------- focus from its central argument.

(A) temerity . . extend
(B) limit . . shift
(C) breadth . . divert
(D) meagerness . . deter
(E) consistency . . detract

18. Experimental research suggests that ------- fearful memories while people are asleep may paradoxically ------- the memories' effects, diminishing their intrusion into waking life.

(A) conjuring . . emancipate
(B) evoking . . mitigate
(C) expelling . . decrease
(D) inducing . . integrate
(E) eliciting . . exacerbate

19. After it was discovered that the city council member had used public funds to pay for personal expenses, he was ------- by his -------.

(A) lauded . . partisans
(B) fortified . . pundits
(C) mollified . . colleagues
(D) censured . . delegates
(E) ousted . . constituents

20. Vita Sackville-West's youthful literary output was -------: by the age of eighteen, she had completed eight historical novels, five plays, and a large number of poems.

(A) renowned
(B) perceptive
(C) reclusive
(D) prodigious
(E) despondent

21. Although the fear of wolves is -------, present in virtually all human societies, wolf attacks are actually quite ------ and only occur when an animal is sick or provoked.

(A) imminent . . anomalous
(B) ubiquitous . . sporadic
(C) endemic . . tragic
(D) inevitable . . devastating
(E) comprehensible . . mundane

22. Sounds dominate the poem so much that the words themselves seem almost -------; however, they are ultimately ------- to its meaning.

(A) trite . . peripheral
(B) central . . attributed
(C) irrelevant . . redundant
(D) arbitrary . . essential
(E) cryptic . . related

23. Some linguists insist that no particular dialect can be considered standard because language is not -------; on the contrary, it is constantly in -------.

(A) stable . . retreat
(B) explicit . . action
(C) immutable . . flux
(D) capricious . . motion
(E) unintelligible . . demand

24. In spite of its shortcomings, the biography of Duke Ellington is redeemed by the author's ------- his subject and his well-supported ------- that Ellington is a world-class composer.

(A) enthusiasm for . . delusion
(B) apathy about . . insistence
(C) exuberance for . . conviction
(D) acknowledgment of . . initiation
(E) insight into . . volition

25. Because earthquakes are often triggered by the movement of magma within a volcano, they are often seen as ------- of disaster, indicating that a major eruption is -------.

(A) paragons . . inevitable
(B) defects . . plausible
(C) expulsions . . catastrophic
(D) catalysts . . inert
(E) harbingers . . imminent

26. Although the author claimed that his book recounted events with great -------, detractors accused him of viewing the truth as ------- and shaping it to advance his own agenda.

(A) detail . . infallible
(B) fidelity . . malleable
(C) exaggeration . . paramount
(D) candor . . reciprocal
(E) interest . . execrable

27. Ghost towns may be created when land is ------- by a government for environmental or military purposes, requiring residents to move elsewhere.

(A) cultivated
(B) interrupted
(C) maintained
(D) expropriated
(E) stipulated

28. Journalist Helen Thomas's ------- for asking blunt questions made her a controversial figure in the world of Washington politics.

(A) disdain
(B) antipathy
(C) proclivity .
(D) abhorrence
(E) disregard

29. Kian is an ------- chess player: he is able to anticipate his opponents' moves well in advance and rarely loses a match.

    (A) adroit
    (B) evasive
    (C) execrable
    (D) unrepentant
    (E) ambitious

30. Linguists sometimes feel discomfort when inventing scripts for traditionally oral languages because the very idea of an alphabet ------- the language and converts the inventor from observer to -------.

    (A) preserves . . participant
    (B) adapts . . bystander
    (C) mimics . . facilitator
    (D) alters . . activist
    (E) explicates . . analyst

31. Michael Crichton's novels ------- the techno-thriller genre, exploring the failures and catastrophes that result from human interaction with biotechnology.

    (A) forestall
    (B) sanctify
    (C) mandate
    (D) jettison
    (E) epitomize

32. Orchestra members were taken aback by the ------- of the conductor's comments; he made no attempt to soften his criticism.

    (A) timorousness
    (B) banality
    (C) diffidence
    (D) callousness
    (E) inscrutability

33. Despite his role as the head of an international fashion empire, Christian Fabré leads an ------- existence, subsisting with only the most basic necessities.

    (A) exalted
    (B) irascible
    (C) egotistical
    (D) oblivious
    (E) ascetic

34. Accustomed as they were to the radio talk-show host's -------, listeners were nonetheless unprepared for the ------- of his most recent tirade.

    (A) diatribes . . vitriol
    (B) foibles . . dogmatism
    (C) punditry . . ideology
    (D) platitudes . . rancor
    (E) idiosyncrasies . . stridency

35. Because Kevin has a tendency to speak -------, he often makes comments that are embarrassingly -------.

    (A) judiciously . . pedantic
    (B) impetuously . . inapt
    (C) philosophically . . phlegmatic
    (D) whimsically . . portentous
    (E) belligerently . . sagacious

Hard (Answers p. 94)

1. In the past, maps often reflected the ------- perspectives of their creators, but the use of computers and satellites to ensure accuracy has rendered them increasingly -------.

   (A) myriad . . superfluous
   (B) eclectic . . uniform
   (C) geographical . . anachronistic
   (D) arbitrary . . recondite
   (E) discrete . . heterogeneous

2. Malthus argued that populations left ------- expand so far beyond the limits of their resources that a crisis inevitably reduces them to a more ------- size.

   (A) fallow . . adaptable
   (B) unchecked . . sustainable
   (C) vulnerable . . robust
   (D) inveterate . . diminutive
   (E) unconstrained . . ample

3. The existence of the Higgs boson particle was traditionally ------- by many scientists; only recently has the notion that the particle is real gained widespread -------.

   (A) impugned . . dexterity
   (B) lauded . . acceptance
   (C) disputed . . traction
   (D) exacerbated . . appreciation
   (E) assuaged . . reticence

4. Rabindrinath Tagore succeed in modernizing Bengali art by ------- the rigid classical forms whose influence had ------- previous attempts at creativity and innovation.

   (A) restoring . . enhanced
   (B) illuminating . . chastised
   (C) eschewing . . frustrated
   (D) undermining . . ameliorated
   (E) prevaricating . . stifled

5. The second century mapmaker Ptolemy was ------- to the biggest and most insidious cartographic -------: when he lacked information, he simply made things up.

   (A) averse . . shortcoming
   (B) subject . . illusion
   (C) related . . achievement
   (D) prone . . vice
   (E) devoted . . anachronism

6. When astronaut Peggy Whitson completed more than 32 hours of space walks in 2007, she ------- the record of 29 hours set by Sunita Williams the previous year.

   (A) admonished
   (B) eclipsed
   (C) scrutinized
   (D) expedited
   (E) obfuscated

7. Though twins, Ramon and Diana have contrasting personalities: Ramon is typically ------- while Diana is -------.

   (A) capricious . . wistful
   (B) diffident . . supercilious
   (C) reserved . . laconic
   (D) taciturn . . gregarious
   (E) credulous . . voluble

8. As a provider of nourishment and natural materials, the coconut tree is ------- resource: a single tree produces up to 6,000 fruits that can be used in hundreds of foods and other essential items.

   (A) an invaluable
   (B) an arboreal
   (C) a trivial
   (D) an ineffable
   (E) an auspicious

9. ------- of genetic crop modification argue that it could help provide sustenance for fast-growing populations by creating foods ------- to pests.

   (A) Analysts . . indifferent
   (B) Perpetrators . . resistant
   (C) Skeptics . . noxious
   (D) Proponents . . invulnerable
   (E) Facilitators . . inconsequential

10. George Orwell was widely ------- for his novella *Animal Farm*, but it was the publication of *1984* that truly ------- his place in literary history.

    (A) misconstrued . . advocated
    (B) reviled . . vindicated
    (C) lauded . . jeopardized
    (D) panned . . insinuated
    (E) extolled . . cemented

11. In response to the candidate's attempt to present herself as -------, her opponents denounced her public displays of generosity as nothing but political -------.

    (A) an ideologue . . dogmatism
    (B) a jingoist . . subterfuge
    (C) an idealist . . authoritarianism
    (D) a mercenary . . partisanship
    (E) an altruist . . machination

12. Sara's ability to mimic her friends is ------; her impressions are so convincing that one cannot help but be ------- while watching them.

    (A) mendacious . . captivated
    (B) bellicose . . enraptured
    (C) virtuosic . . assuaged
    (D) preternatural . . unnerved
    (E) ineluctable . . disquieted

13. Unlike other authors, who portray the security officers at Robert Oppenheimer's laboratory as either mindless bureaucrats or paranoid witch-hunters, Ray Monk offers a much more ------- depiction.

    (A) nuanced
    (B) perfunctory
    (C) consummate
    (D) bellicose
    (E) illustrious

14. Willa Cather's novels are often viewed reverently as the embodiment of life in the American Midwest, but this ------- view conflicts with the reality that Cather was a ------- writer.

    (A) spurious . . pejorative
    (B) provincial . . didactic
    (C) exclusive . . recondite
    (D) myopic . . compelling
    (E) parochial . . cosmopolitan

15. Once ------- proponent of reform, the administrator now ------- the very institutional changes she once sought to implement.

    (A) a fervid . . evokes
    (B) a torpid . . vituperates
    (C) an ardent . . excoriates
    (D) an elusive . . ostracizes
    (E) an unswerving . . promulgates

16. Believing she was no longer suited for the role, the actress gave little thought to rejecting it; however, she later reconsidered, worried that she had acted too -------.

    (A) apprehensively
    (B) precipitously
    (C) zealously
    (D) parsimoniously
    (E) duplicitously

17. Critics' praise for the artist was -------: it was entirely unmarred by any unfavorable commentary.

   (A) tacit
   (B) blithe
   (C) trivial
   (D) unqualified
   (E) convoluted

18. In *The Idealist*, Nina Munk presents her subject as -------, holding fiercely to his ideals and unwilling to ------- any flaws in their implementation.

   (A) tenacious . . burnish
   (B) exalted . . undermine
   (C) intransigent . . concede
   (D) obdurate . . expurgate
   (E) inscrutable . . recognize

19. Even though some of the Algonquin Round Table's contemporaries ------- the group during its existence, its reputation has remained mostly ------- since its dissolution in 1929.

   (A) ignored . . inconsequential
   (B) savaged . . unscathed
   (C) assuaged . . definitive
   (D) scoffed at . . cryptic
   (E) censured . . unexceptional

20. Some critics have accused Dorothy Sayers' novels of being ------- because many of their characters seem to ------- directly from the author's own life rather than her imagination.

   (A) auspicious . . seep
   (B) ephemeral . . derive
   (C) derivative . . stem
   (D) timorous . . exude
   (E) individualistic . . abscond

21. Observing that their experiment was failing to ------- any significant data, the researchers chose to ------- it until they could determine a more effective methodology.

   (A) stipulate . . postpone
   (B) display . . assuage
   (C) yield . . table
   (D) emit . . ostracize
   (E) withhold . . jettison

22. The senator was notorious for his ------- speeches, but colleagues dismissed his overblown rhetoric as nothing but -------.

   (A) caustic . . chicanery
   (B) sensationalistic . . diffidence
   (C) pretentious . . subjectivity
   (D) ponderous . . arrogance
   (E) bombastic . . bluster

23. While the venom of a few spiders species has ------- effects on humans, it also has curative properties that can be ------- for use in medications and non-toxic pesticides

   (A) soporific . . stimulated
   (B) adverse . . exploited
   (C) mollifying . . constrained
   (D) unanticipated . . elicited
   (E) palliative . . diagnosed

24. Lucinda is -------: even when clearly mistaken, she avoids ------- anyone else's point of view.

   (A) capricious . . ruminating on
   (B) obstinate . . acquiescing to
   (C) equivocal . . genuflecting to
   (D) quiescent . . deferring to
   (E) tractable . . engaging with

25. Although Benjamin Barber and Pierre
    Manent's studies of urbanism contain similar
    theses, the former seems -------, even callow,
    while the latter is a work of profound -------.

    (A) meticulous . . fastidiousness
    (B) superficial . . buoyancy
    (C) naïve . . atonement
    (D) terse . . obsequiousness
    (E) ingenuous . . erudition

Set 1 (Answers p. 99)

1. Native to the Galapagos Islands, the giant tortoise is known for its extraordinary -------: it can live to be well over 100 years old.

   (A) amplitude
   (B) longevity
   (C) graciousness
   (D) severity
   (E) sluggishness

2. The theory of pragmatism resulted from the belief that ideas should not be viewed as abstract truths but rather judged by their   -   ------ consequences.

   (A) immediate
   (B) severe
   (C) felicitous
   (D) practical
   (E) unintentional

3. Around 400 A.D., the Andean civilization of Tiwanaku shifted from a locally dominant force to ------- state, one that conquered its neighbors and ------- its culture widely.

   (A) an influential . . evaluated
   (B) a monarchical . . inflicted
   (C) a powerful . . subsumed
   (D) a democratic . . distributed
   (E) an imperialist . . disseminated

4. A scientist, surveyor, almanac author and farmer, Benjamin Banneker was also -------: he had little formal education and was largely self-taught.

   (A) a pedant
   (B) an autodidact
   (C) an extrovert
   (D) a pacifist
   (E) a charlatan

5. Characterized by a detached and ------ style, the author's new novel lacks the sort of emotional ------- that her readers have come to expect.

   (A) diffident . . reticent
   (B) hackneyed . . scrutiny
   (C) aloof . . poignancy
   (D) convoluted . . diligence
   (E) analytical . . vapidity

Set 2 (Answers p. 100)

1. Around 10,000 years ago, early hunter-gatherers began to make ------- stone tools, but as more sophisticated technologies developed, their creations became increasingly -------.

   (A) fragile . . enigmatic
   (B) simple . . elusive
   (C) impressive . . debased
   (D) primitive . . complex
   (E) elaborate . . refined

2. Janacek's mature compositions represent a highly original -------- of styles because they ------- musical traditions that developed independently of one another for centuries.

   (A) synthesis . . integrate
   (B) diffusion . . combine
   (C) amalgam . . delineate
   (D) combination . . undermine
   (E) cacophony . . blend

3. American newspapers publish editorials on their front pages ------- and only for topics of unusual importance; in other countries, however, the practice is much more -------.

   (A) cautiously . . deliberate
   (B) impulsively . . popular
   (C) belatedly . . typical
   (D) sporadically . . frequent
   (E) continuously . . innovative

4. Seen from the mountaintop, the frost-blue lake and cloudless sky created ------- image of beauty and calm, one so stunning that it could not be fully captured in words.

(A) a churlish
(B) an ineffable
(C) a monumental
(D) a prescient
(E) an ominous

5. Linguist Noam Chomsky has theorized that all languages are built on an underlying universal grammar, an assertion that is not only ------- but downright -------.

(A) erudite . . inane
(B) nebulous . . lucid
(C) fortuitous . . quixotic
(D) contentious . . polemical
(E) myopic . . pedantic

Set 3 (Answers p. 101)

1. The essence of jazz is -------; no other genre of music relies so much on the art of composing in the moment.

(A) cacophony
(B) improvisation
(C) exhibitionism
(D) recapitulation
(E) collaboration

2. William Jennings Bryan's speech at the 1896 Democratic National Convention ------- his supporters, breathing new life into a campaign that had previously been quite staid.

(A) dissuaded
(B) galvanized — energized
(C) obligated
(D) perpetuated
(E) enfranchised

3. The Arco lamp's ------- appearance is the result of its ------- design: the unexpected juxtaposition of forms and materials creates an impression that is entirely unique.

(A) innocuous . . whimsical
(B) distinctive . . eclectic
(C) uncanny . . lustrous
(D) unusual . . pedestrian
(E) striking . . utilitarian

4. The masks used in Greek tragedy were -------- objects: they were made of organic materials, and no physical evidence of them survives today.

(A) decorous — decorate
(B) picturesque
(C) ephemeral — Short-lived
(D) monstrous
(E) sacred

5. The Roman historian Plutarch rarely touched on serious events, recounting ------- incidents because he believed that they revealed more about his subjects than their more ------- accomplishments did.

(A) frivolous . . classical
(B) apocryphal . . grandiose
(C) serene . . insolent
(D) trivial . . venerable
(E) austere . . ostensible

Set 4 (Answers p. 102)

1. Mitsuko Uchida is one of the most ------- pianists of her generation: she has appeared with most of the world's foremost orchestras and won numerous international awards.

(A) musical
(B) flamboyant
(C) acclaimed
(D) unnerving
(E) versatile

2. Contrary to popular belief, the British government did not respond ------- to the news of the Boston Tea Party but rather -------- at length about the consequences of its reaction.

(A) cautiously . . expounded
(B) impulsively . . deliberated
(C) intentionally . . debated
(D) diplomatically . . discussed
(E) prudently . . finagled

3. In spite of their obvious physical advantages, bears almost never view humans as prey and rarely behave in a ------- manner toward them.

(A) magnanimous
(B) conniving
(C) timid
(D) bellicose — *agressive*
(E) capricious

nothing to do w/ agressive

4. While physics and art may outwardly appear to have little in common, they do have some ------- similarities because both are grounded in mathematical principles.

not disturbing → hidden

(A) latent
(B) essential
(C) trivial
(D) misleading
(E) tacit

5. The city's growth has been ------- by a law ------- the construction of new buildings within the city limits.

(A) mitigated . . encouraging
(B) restricted . . converging
(C) facilitated . . curtailing
(D) exculpated . . simplifying
(E) circumscribed . . restricting

Set 5 (Answers p. 103)

1. In a state of disrepair when it was discovered in 1911, the city of Macchu Pichu has now been partially ------- to its original appearance.

(A) inspired
(B) commanded
(C) restored
(D) targeted
(E) revealed

2. Intended to be discarded after a single use, the Dixie Cup was created by public health workers order to ------- the ------- of diseases at public water sources.

(A) abolish . . prognosis
(B) stimulate . . outbreak
(C) diagnose . . occurrence
(D) identify . . restriction
(E) mitigate . . transmission

3. In many ancient dwellings, the most important rooms were placed near the entrance; in contrast, ------- spaces were ------- to the back and reserved for storage.

(A) ancillary . . relegated
(B) luminous . . resigned
(C) contemporary . . demoted
(D) flexible . . distributed
(E) cavernous . . consigned

4. Scott Turow's courtroom thrillers are often cited for their ------- appeal: their thrilling and suspenseful plots immediately elicit intense emotions.

(A) phlegmatic
(B) dubious
(C) visceral
(D) implacable
(E) explicit

50

5. Accused of ------- by her opponent, the candidate protested that, on the contrary, she had always been entirely -------.

(A) dissent . . elusive
(B) obfuscation . . frank
(C) diplomacy . . diffident
(D) profiteering . . surreptitious
(E) duplicitousness . . terse

Set 6 (Answers p. 104)

1. Although it was popularized in the twentieth century, the yo-yo actually has ------- roots: it was invented in Greece sometime around 500 B.C.

(A) obscure
(B) diverse
(C) unexpected
(D) ancient
(E) fascinating

2. Copernicus developed his theory of heliocentrism entirely without experimentation, but it was eventually ------- because his descriptions of planetary motion were more ------- than his predecessors'.

(A) rejected . . intriguing
(B) permitted . . trivial
(C) embraced . . convincing
(D) deduced . . imaginative
(E) jettisoned . . arrogant

3. Although it is spoken by fewer than 250,000 people, the Tuvan language is ------- in comparison to its more ------- counterparts, some of which have only a few remaining speakers.

(A) fragile . . delicate
(B) banal . . loquacious
(C) vital . . aberrant
(D) robust . . tenuous
(E) ambiguous . . esoteric

4. Renzo Piano earned a reputation as ------- for his design of the Pompidou Center, whose exterior of brightly colored tubes marked a radical break with architectural tradition.

(A) a reactionary
(B) an aesthete
(C) a maverick
(D) an indigent
(E) a cosmopolitan

5. Despite his penchant for stubbornness, even -------, Edmund Burke won fame for the brilliance and ------- of his political writings.

(A) intractability . . eloquence
(B) obtuseness . . lucidity
(C) alacrity . . munificence
(D) resilience . . perspicacity
(E) intransigence . . vapidity

Set 7 (Answers p. 105)

1. Frederick Law Olmsted believed that a city's green space should be equally accessible to all its citizens, and his design of Central Park embodied that ------- ideal.

(A) colossal
(B) distant
(C) egalitarian
(D) urban
(E) pastoral

2. Many children are -------- unfamiliar foods and will only try a new dish after they have been offered it ten or more times.

(A) enthusiastic about
(B) curious about
(C) delighted by
(D) wary of
(E) enthralled by

3. Because air creates a ------- formation, with cooler layers sinking and warmer ones rising above them, ceiling fans are often used to heat rooms by ------- the warm from the ceiling toward the floor.

(A) hypnotic . . elevating
(B) stratified . . circulating
(C) convoluted . . shifting
(D) vacuous . . declining
(E) transitory . . redirecting

4. The company's ------- of the market is so complete that its brand name has become virtually ------- the product itself.

(A) domination . . abhorred by
(B) appraisal . . confused with
(C) monopolization . . synonymous with
(D) embodiment . . surpassed by
(E) abandonment . . captivated by

5. The origin of heavy metals such as gold and platinum is source of debate among astronomers, but one theory suggests that they were ------- by collisions between stars.

(A) collated
(B) forged
(C) desiccated
(D) oriented
(E) propelled

Set 8 (Answers p. 106)

1. Realizing that they had nearly ------- their supplies, the hikers decided to cut short their journey and return to camp.

(A) emaciated
(B) abducted
(C) exported
(D) replenished
(E) depleted

2. The Spanish Empire was not a ------- monarchy with one legal system but a federation of ------- realms, each jealously guarding its own rights.

(A) heterogeneous . . diverse
(B) united . . discrete
(C) constitutional . . variegated
(D) conservative . . constituent
(E) absolutist . . populous

3. Animals that live on islands are ------- to unforeseen environmental disasters because their possibilities for escape are limited.

(A) vulnerable
(B) indifferent
(C) inured
(D) insensitive
(E) crucial

4. The biographer often adopts a ------- tone: he discusses incidents for their moral lessons rather than simply describing their historical significance.

(A) didactic
(B) inflexible
(C) conciliatory
(D) recondite
(E) flippant

5. Isabella Stewart Gardner's ------- for eccentricity as well as her tendency to ------- social conventions made her the subject of much gossip.

(A) disdain . . reject
(B) enthusiasm . . embrace
(C) predilection . . grasp
(D) penchant . . flout
(E) aptitude . . condone

Set 9 (Answers p. 106)

1. Grizzly bears are usually ------- animals, but they ------- in groups alongside rivers when salmon come to spawn.

   (A) intimidating . . multiply
   (B) noble . . locate
   (C) devious . . scatter
   (D) solitary . . congregate
   (E) curious . . commiserate

2. Although the term "banana" refers to a soft, sweet fruit, while "plantain" refers to a firmer, starchier one, they are genetically identical, so the distinction between them is largely -------.

   (A) adaptive
   (B) biological
   (C) arbitrary
   (D) profound
   (E) arcane

3. The author's novels, once highly original, have become ------- ; they simply recycle themes and plotlines from his earlier works.

   (A) pessimistic
   (B) intriguing
   (C) derivative
   (D) prurient
   (E) succinct

4. Though valued for their delicate flavor, shrimp are actually ------- creatures that have a high tolerance for the toxins found in polluted waters.

   (A) benign
   (B) auspicious
   (C) hardy
   (D) voracious
   (E) aquatic

5. Lie detector tests have failed to gain ------- among scientists because they are easily ------- by people experienced at controlling their emotions.

   (A) credibility . . exonerated
   (B) suspicion . . deceived
   (C) interest . . improved
   (D) currency . . duped
   (E) popularity . . imitated

Set 10 (Answers p. 107)

1. In recent years, researchers have made large strides toward stamping out the disease, encouraging them to believe that it may soon be ------- entirely.

   (A) understood
   (B) excluded
   (C) detected
   (D) contained
   (E) eradicated

2. Historically, societies have developed methods of ------- their lifestyles to fit their environments, with acquired behaviors eventually becoming ------- customs.

   (A) altering . . peripheral
   (B) creating . . deleterious
   (C) adapting . . ingrained
   (D) modifying . . ingenious
   (E) verifying . . essential

3. The Milky Way galaxy's name ------- its appearance as a solid milky white band in which individual stars cannot be -------.

   (A) belies . . measured
   (B) precludes . . observed
   (C) reflects . . distinguished
   (D) scrutinizes . . pinpointed
   (E) determines . . identified

4. Of more than 50,000 dietary supplements on the market, only a few have proven -------, with the popularity of the rest a ------- to the power of self-delusion.

   (A) benefits . . testament
   (B) effects . . comparison
   (C) components . . prescription
   (D) nutrients . . refutation
   (E) caveats . . recommendation

5. While mental telepathy has been a staple of science fiction novels for decades, scientific consensus dismisses it as pure -------.

   (A) alacrity
   (B) chicanery
   (C) publicity
   (D) tenacity
   (E) monotony

Set 11 (Answers p. 108)

1. Hogans, square or octagonal wooden structures covered in mud, are ------- the Navajo people; they are built by no other Native American tribe.

   (A) identical to
   (B) vulnerable to
   (C) dependent on
   (D) unique to
   (E) appreciated by

2. Theodore Roosevelt used his presidential powers to create over 150 national forests, an achievement that was ------- by the more ------- efforts of arborists who planted trees in cities and parks.

   (A) deterred . . invasive
   (B) defined . . prosaic
   (C) supplemented . . modest
   (D) obliterated . . exaggerated
   (E) amplified . . exclusive

3. Although the language of the Declaration of Independence is remarkably -------, the florid eighteenth century handwriting can be difficult for modern readers to -------.

   (A) forthright . . extol
   (B) ineffable . . comprehend
   (C) dense . . initiate
   (D) lucid . . decipher
   (E) convoluted . . discern

4. Mostly known for his depictions of ------- London streets, Dickens was equally inspired by the far more ------- mountains of the Swiss countryside.

   (A) bustling . . fastidious
   (B) placid . . idyllic
   (C) gritty . . bucolic
   (D) tranquil . . serene
   (E) chaotic . . irreverent

5. The scientist's work, once widely praised, is now being ------- in some quarters as the ------- of shoddiness.

   (A) attacked . . antithesis
   (B) pilloried . . epitome
   (C) extolled . . ideal
   (D) probed . . corroboration
   (E) disputed . . forerunner

Set 12 (Answers p. 109)

1. The Bauhaus school was founded with the goal of creating a ------- work of art, one in which all art forms would eventually be brought together.

   (A) durable
   (B) peculiar
   (C) renowned
   (D) stunning
   (E) comprehensive

2. Ancient documents imply that Darius the Great ------- the heir to the Persian throne by force and seized it for himself, indicating that his rise to power was most likely -------.

(A) deposed . . illicit
(B) defended . . laudable
(C) subjugated . . benevolent
(D) supplanted . . cursory
(E) appeased . . illegitimate

3. While social ------- do exist among bonobo chimpanzees, rank plays a less ------- role in their societies than it does in other primate societies.

(A) structures . . elusive
(B) restrictions . . creative
(C) hierarchies . . prominent
(D) institutions . . generic
(E) relations . . ambiguous

4. The multiple perspectives presented in Siri Hustvedt's novel do not ------- into a single view but rather create an atmosphere of ------- and flux.

(A) coalesce . . rigidity
(B) palliate . . obsequiousness
(C) merge . . profundity
(D) evade . . profligacy
(E) cohere . . ambiguity

5. Soap operas are often cited for their outrageous plotlines and wooden acting, but some media scholars argue that they provide -------, even ------- societal commentary.

(A) insightful . . decorous
(B) astute . . prosaic
(C) sharp . . trenchant
(D) lucid . . sanctimonious
(E) reserved . . caustic

Set 13 (Answers p. 110)

1. Supporters of the new law are requesting that it be -------- as slowly as possible in order to give those affected the time to -------.

(A) implemented . . adapt
(B) introduced . . revolt
(C) overturned . . protest
(D) described . . react
(E) abolished . . adjust

2. Because novelist Milan Kundera considers his characters' external appearances ------- his stories, he often spends little time describing their appearances.

(A) peripheral to
(B) skeptical about
(C) reliant on
(D) indispensable to
(E) imbued with

3. The same forces that drive people to consume more resources can also push them toward -------: seeing their neighbors conserve energy makes them more environmentally ------- as well.

(A) delinquency . . responsible
(B) sustainability . . conscious
(C) objectivity . . adept
(D) responsibility . . apathetic
(E) creativity . . aware

4. Often overlooked by the public is the tendency for scientists to publish their singular successes and ignore their multiple failures, making a ------- look like ------- discovery.

(A) calculation. . an intentional
(B) resolution . . a perceptive
(C) fluke . . a deliberate
(D) goal . . a groundbreaking
(E) complication . . a problematic

5. Margaret Thatcher was nicknamed the Iron Lady because of her ------- and ------- style of leadership.

   (A) determination . . mercurial
   (B) obstinacy . . unyielding
   (C) acquiescence . . contentious
   (D) tenacity . . conciliatory
   (E) firmness . . cavalier

Set 14 (Answers p. 111)

1. Mount St. Helens is known for its ------- eruption on May 18, 1980, the deadliest and most economically destructive volcanic event in the history of the United States.

   (A) stressful
   (B) catastrophic
   (C) subtle
   (D) unexpected
   (E) continuous

2. To -------- the growing discontent among American colonists, Lord North ------- many of the tariffs imposed by King George III.

   (A) inflame . . destroyed
   (B) quell . . rescinded
   (C) deny . . questioned
   (D) placate . . finalized
   (E) stimulate . . denounced

3. The director earned a reputation for ------- behavior because he harshly ------- any actor who dared to question his instructions.

   (A) magnanimous . . chastised
   (B) compulsive . . criticized
   (C) despotic . . cajoled
   (D) capricious . . defended
   (E) tyrannical . . berated

4. The philosopher John Locke argued that people are born without ------- ideas and that knowledge is -------- from interactions with the physical world.

   (A) tenuous . . acquired
   (B) definitive . . explained
   (C) essential . . obtained
   (D) innate . . derived
   (E) esoteric . . applied

5. While the novel undoubtedly contains some ------- elements, it is at the same time so full of ------- that it defies any attempt at categorization.

   (A) trite . . platitudes
   (B) unexpected . . soliloquies
   (C) prosaic . . innuendos
   (D) theoretical . . abstractions
   (E) hackneyed . . idiosyncrasies

Set 15 (Answers p. 112)

1. The scientist has been repeatedly criticized for refusing to ------- his theory, even when confronted with facts that clearly ------- its flaws.

   (A) debate . . challenge
   (B) promote . . reveal
   (C) abandon . . demonstrate
   (D) simplify . . undermine
   (E) relinquish . . manipulate

2. Most people refer to the tomato as a vegetable, but that is a -------; in fact, the word tomato comes from the Nahuatl word "tomatl," the swelling fruit.

   (A) misnomer
   (B) panacea
   (C) distraction
   (D) hypothesis
   (E) detriment

3. While much of the soil in Australia lacks nutrients, the country's many trees and lush plant life ------- the first European settlers into ------- its potential for food production.

(A) seduced . . denying
(B) intimidated . . condemning
(C) deceived . . overestimating
(D) misled . . contemplating
(E) delighted . . defending

4. While many cultures have view sharks as ------- beasts, ones that live in close association with the sea tend regard them with respect, even -------.

(A) voracious . . reticence
(B) chimerical . . admiration
(C) rapacious . . reverence
(D) demonic . . remuneration
(E) magnanimous . . perplexity

5. Novelist Saul Bellow's early style was ------ if rarely -------: it reflected his keen sense of observation but was entirely lacking in economy of expression.

(A) descriptive . . prosaic
(B) unwavering . . contrite
(C) ironic . . facetious
(D) perspicacious . . laconic
(E) bemusing . . succinct

Set 16 (Answers p. 113)

1. A lizard that loses its tail can partially ------- the limb, although the new section will often contain cartilage rather than bone.

(A) preserve
(B) select
(C) regenerate
(D) define
(E) strengthen

2. In the past, scientific progress was often -------, but recent technological advances have permitted scientists to rapidly make many breakthroughs.

(A) experimental
(B) fortuitous
(C) collaborative
(D) incremental
(E) controversial

3. Known for his ------- personality, the poet was infamously ------- of social gatherings and preferred to spend his time alone.

(A) insufferable . . mindful
(B) aloof . . defensive
(C) flamboyant . . fearful
(D) taciturn . . aware
(E) misanthropic . . chary

4. Although the Incas wanted to extend their empire into Chile, the native Mapuche people refused to -------, successfully ------- the Incas' attempts to conquer them.

(A) capitulate . . thwarting
(B) resist . . repudiating
(C) attack . . outwitting
(D) acquiesce . . emancipating
(E) exculpating . . contending

5. Ernest Hemingway's admission that he rewrote the ending of *A Farewell to Arms* thirty-nine times set a ------- for ------- that few writers since have come close to matching.

(A) standard . . equivocation
(B) fashion . . stoicism
(C) course . . punditry
(D) precedent . . scrupulousness
(E) paradigm . . discretion

Set 17 (Answers p. 113)

1. There are so many ------- accounts of the extinct dodo bird's appearance that its exact appearance is a -------.

    (A) conflicting . . mystery
    (B) deliberate . . template
    (C) vivid . . debate
    (D) precise . . curiosity
    (E) similar . . digression

2. Doris Lessing has earned wide acclaim for her ability to ------- complex issues, to examine them closely and from multiple perspectives.

    (A) gratify
    (B) scrutinize
    (C) exonerate
    (D) moderate
    (E) contrive

3. Citrus greening disease, which can ------- entire groves in only a few months, has become a ------- for orange growers.

    (A) fertilize . . menace
    (B) decimate . . paragon
    (C) corrupt . . quandary
    (D) ravage . . scourge
    (E) repulse . . balm

4. The historian's observations in any given moment are invariably original and -------, yet the lessons he draws from those observations are for the most part ------- and uninspired.

    (A) intelligent . . implicit
    (B) profound . . erudite
    (C) methodical . . irrevocable
    (D) edifying . . formulaic
    (E) supercilious . . pompous

5. Profoundly respectful of the past, painter Dominique Ingres ------- responsibility for guarding academic ------- against the encroaching popularity of the new Romantic style.

    (A) defended . . intuition
    (B) assumed . . orthodoxy
    (C) decried . . provincialism
    (D) accepted . . sophistry
    (E) affirmed . . charlatanism

Set 18 (Answers p. 114)

1. Some scientists predict that the energy industry will be ------- by the drought because oil and gas plants ------- water to function.

    (A) destroyed . . comply with
    (B) improved . . rely on
    (C) attacked . . insist on
    (D) devastated . . depend on
    (E) promoted . . elaborate on

2. Venus Williams ranks among the world's most ------- athletes because she has won more Olympic gold medals than any other female tennis player.

    (A) preeminent
    (B) indefensible
    (C) effusive
    (D) condescending
    (E) benevolent

3. To create successful rides, roller coaster designers must ------- two seemingly contradictory goals: keeping riders safe and creating a terrifying experience.

    (A) reiterate
    (B) ameliorate
    (C) abolish
    (D) reconcile
    (E) excoriate

4. Icebergs, strong winds, and large waves make the waters around Cape Horn extremely -------; only the most ------- sailors dare to navigate them.

(A) turbulent . . incredulous
(B) placid . . intrepid
(C) voracious . . assiduous
(D) torpid . . indignant
(E) perilous . . foolhardy

5. Alex had a tendency to worry about his boss's reactions to his work, but Tameka ------- his concerns as entirely -------.

(A) disdained . . anachronistic
(B) evoked . . prosaic
(C) bolstered . . dogmatic
(D) impugned . . litigious
(E) dismissed . . immaterial

Set 19 (Answers p. 115)

1. It is generally unnecessary to vaccinate children against measles before they are eighteen months old because most have natural ------- until the age of two.

(A) utility
(B) immunity
(C) atrophy
(D) curiosity
(E) infirmity

2. Scientists have long thought that Mars, warm and wet in its early years, could have hosted microorganisms, but new findings suggest that the planet is ------- to life.

(A) inapplicable
(B) endemic
(C) superfluous
(D) inhospitable
(E) affirmative

3. After discovering that the agreed-upon ------- had been eliminated by their managers, the workers ------- on the contract.

(A) stipulations . . reneged
(B) evaluations . . focused
(C) modifications . . depended
(D) caveats . . ruminated
(E) liabilities . . meditated

4. A fundamental scientific question is which of a person's abilities are due to ------- differences in the brain and which are due to ------- factors such as learning and practice.

(A) innate . . congenital
(B) unforeseen . . marginal
(C) intrinsic . . external
(D) structural . . isolated
(E) conscious . . environmental

5. Unhampered by ------- equipment, post-Impressionist painters used some of the first handheld cameras to observe rapid light effects previously too ------- to capture.

(A) sophisticated . . abstruse
(B) anachronistic . . torpid
(C) cumbersome . . fleeting
(D) obstreperous . . cloying
(E) valuable . . cursory

Set 20 (Answers p. 116)

1. As one of 8,000 people to respond to a newspaper advertisement for space program applicants, Sally Ride faced ------- odds.

(A) negligible
(B) impeccable
(C) imaginary
(D) daunting
(E) captivating

2. After World War I, the abolition of censorship in the Weimar Republic allowed -------- of radical experimentation in arts that had been ------- by the old regime.

   (A) a dearth . . expunged
   (B) an excess . . sacrificed
   (C) an influx . . corroborated
   (D) a modicum . . encouraged
   (E) an upsurge . . suppressed

3. Unlike her brother Scott, who has a tendency to -------, Anna is ------- and rarely reconsiders once she has made up her mind.

   (A) procrastinate . . obstinate
   (B) waver . . forthright
   (C) genuflect . . astute
   (D) speculate . . tenacious
   (E) vacillate . . steadfast

4. Puns serve a ------- as well as a ------- purpose: not only do they provide momentary amusement but they also render lessons more vivid and memorable to listeners.

   (A) quixotic . . practical
   (B) frivolous . . didactic
   (C) subtle . . residual
   (D) vital . . descriptive
   (E) diverting . . stabilizing

5. To appease voters angered by her predecessor's -------, the gubernatorial candidate promised that she would implement a policy of fiscal -------.

   (A) judiciousness . . posterity
   (B) coercion . . manipulation
   (C) naiveté . . analysis
   (D) diffidence . . emancipation
   (E) profligacy . . restraint

Set 21 (Answers p. 117)

1. Spanish culture ------- during Phillip II's reign, initiating the Golden Age that left a lasting legacy in literature, music, and the visual arts.

   (A) mellowed
   (B) flourished
   (C) declined
   (D) stagnated
   (E) compounded

2. Watermelon is thought to have originated in Southern Africa, where it often grows wild, but some botanists have suggested that it might be ------- tropical Africa instead.

   (A) associated with
   (B) correlated with
   (C) subdued by
   (D) transferable to
   (E) indigenous to

3. Achieving fluency in a foreign language means abandoning familiar assumptions and immersing oneself in a worldview that may at first seem quite -------.

   (A) analogous
   (B) myopic
   (C) uniform
   (D) trivial
   (E) alien

4. Napoleon's 1812 invasion of Russia was a ------- moment because the French army, once considered invincible, never fully recovered from the damage it withstood in the campaign.

   (A) triumphal
   (B) resolute
   (C) conciliatory
   (D) watershed
   (E) belligerent

5. Although scholars initially suspected that the nearly 200 year-old manuscript, ------- written by a fugitive female slave, was a fraud, the author's identity was eventually   ------- by experts.

(A) assiduously . . impugned
(B) negligibly . . confirmed
(C) impetuously . . alleviated
(D) allegedly . . foreseen
(E) ostensibly . . authenticated

6. Some countries fail spectacularly, with a total ------- of all state institutions, but most do so by being utterly unable to ------- their societies' enormous potential for growth.

(A) acceleration . . revere
(B) collapse . . forestall
(C) revocation . . extirpate
(D) propagation . . unify
(E) disintegration . . tap

Set 22 (Answers p. 118)

1. *Home to Harlem* is considered Claude McKay's most ------- novel because it had a major impact on intellectuals in both the United States and abroad.

(A) poetic
(B) controversial
(C) influential
(D) autobiographical
(E) lucrative

2. In response to growing radicalism, every public official must submit a signed oath of ------- declaring allegiance to the government.

(A) fidelity
(B) judiciousness
(C) subversion
(D) equality
(E) conscription

3. Alan Turing not only ------- the possibility of building a computer but he also showed exactly how the construction of such a machine was -------.

(A) imagined . . ludicrous
(B) classified . . imminent
(C) predicted . . impractical
(D) decried . . plausible
(E) intuited . . feasible

4. While most leaf forms are structured to maximize the absorption of sunlight, a minority have adapted to ------- the amount of light they absorb and ------- exposure to excessive heat.

(A) reduce . . aggravate
(B) stimulate . . limit
(C) expand . . attenuate
(D) moderate . . mitigate
(E) inhibit . . substantiate

5. Although B.F. Skinner is considered a pioneer in the field of psychology, his ideas have recently been ------- as destructive, even morally -------.

(A) perceived . . bankrupt
(B) maligned . . edifying
(C) simulated . . gratifying
(D) extolled . . corrupt
(E) denigrated . . astute

6. At the end of his career, the psychologist became fascinated with psychics and other mystical phenomena, an interest that his more ------- colleagues dismissed as -------.

(A) subdued . . charlatanism
(B) hesitant . . impudence
(C) incredulous. . quackery
(D) astute . . punditry
(E) skeptical . . coercion

Set 23 (Answers p. 119)

1. Authors of autobiographies often ------- unflattering behaviors in order to present themselves in the best possible light.

    (A) imitate
    (B) downplay
    (C) endorse
    (D) resolve
    (E) accentuate

2. The buildings of Persepolis were famed for their wooden columns: builders ------- stone only when Lebanese cedar or Indian teak could not be -------.

    (A) descended to . . apprehended
    (B) relied on . . created
    (C) resorted to . . obtained
    (D) intruded on . . found
    (E) depended on . . captured

3. Though high and imposing, the Alps do not form an ------- barrier; they were ------- by soldiers and merchants during Roman times, and later by pilgrims, students, and tourists.

    (A) unquestionable . . pillaged
    (B) impassable . . affirmed
    (C) inscrutable . . invoked
    (D) insurmountable . . traversed
    (E) uncouth . . trampled

4. Progress in developing more effective global health programs has been ------- by the ------- of systematic large-scale approaches to improving program design.

    (A) accelerated . . destruction
    (B) diminished . . proliferation
    (C) hindered . . paucity
    (D) obstructed . . popularity
    (E) ameliorated . . dearth

5. Inspired by his friendship with Tchaikovsky, Alexander Glazunov ------- his artistic outlook beyond a nationalist agenda and began to compose along more ------- themes.

    (A) expanded . . contemporary
    (B) restrained . . universal
    (C) inculcated . . grandiose
    (D) broadened . . cosmopolitan
    (E) remonstrated . . mellifluous

6. Although Chandra did her best to remain -------, it was clear from her expression that she was ------- by the unexpected news.

    (A) irate . . bemused
    (B) alert . . flustered
    (C) stoic . . unperturbed
    (D) composed . . nonplussed
    (E) engaged . . mesmerized

Set 24 (Answers p. 121)

1. Some popular dishes have so many -------- that even people within the same city cannot agree on how they should be prepared.

    (A) variations
    (B) descriptions
    (C) flavors
    (D) critics
    (E) ingredients

2. Grapefruit juice interacts dangerously with many common medications; only a few sips can turn a ------- dose into one that is -------.

    (A) beneficial . . reactive
    (B) therapeutic . . toxic
    (C) prescriptive . . harmful
    (D) detrimental . . noxious
    (E) curative . . salutary

3. The renowned painter often behaved unpleasantly, but his actions were ------- by others because of his ------- abilities.

    (A) condoned . . virtuosic
    (B) minimized . . dubious
    (C) overlooked . . mundane
    (D) abused . . musical
    (E) chastised . . impressive

4. When average temperatures increase very slowly, it becomes difficult to notice the difference in baseline standards for normalcy because the shift is all but --------.

    (A) advantageous
    (B) imperceptible
    (C) catastrophic
    (D) undeniable
    (E) naturalistic

5. Dorothy Parker's biting wit earned her great fame, but she was eventually fired from Vanity Fair because the magazine's editors disapproved of her excessively ------- style.

    (A) timorous
    (B) convoluted
    (C) hackneyed
    (D) florid
    (E) caustic

6. Georgia O'Keefe's ability to paint was ------- by vision problems toward the end of her career, but she -------, working in pencil and charcoal until she was more than ninety years old.

    (A) rectified . . procrastinated
    (B) marred . . deviated
    (C) complemented . . persisted
    (D) averted . . commemorated
    (E) compromised . . persevered

Set 25 (Answers p. 122)

1. The Olympic games were banned in A.D. 393 by Theodosius I, but Europeans continued to hold them in spite of that -------.

    (A) prohibition
    (B) delay
    (C) embellishment
    (D) rebellion
    (E) threat

2. While Kepler was the first person to ------- a system that correctly described planetary motion, he did not succeed in ------- a complete theory.

    (A) invent . . refuting
    (B) imagine . . overturning
    (C) disprove . . validating
    (D) devise . . formulating
    (E) develop . . revoking

3. Reading has historically been an exclusive exchange between the reader and the words on the page, but interactive technologies have transformed it into a far less ------- activity.

    (A) comprehensive
    (B) isolated
    (C) intense
    (D) collaborative
    (E) nostalgic

4. For decades, the concept of supersymmetry has been one of the biggest ------- in modern physics, having repeatedly ------- scientists' attempts at understanding.

    (A) enigmas . . confirmed
    (B) theorems . . subdued
    (C) conundrums . . stymied
    (D) hypotheses . . obscured
    (E) predicaments . . foretold

5. Some critics have suggested that the author's study of anthropology ------- his literary style, and indeed, anthropological references often ------- his works.

(A) influenced . . maintain
(B) demeaned . . pervade
(C) informed . . pepper
(D) challenged . . fill
(E) determined . . coddle

6. Standing aloof from academic squabbles, the writer is able to discuss complex debates in a clear and ------- manner that is remarkably free of insider -------.

(A) ingenuous . . euphemism
(B) unequivocal . . admonition
(C) supercilious . . contingency
(D) lucid . . jargon
(E) precise . . alacrity

Set 26 (Answers p. 123)

1. Mary Wollstonecraft's ------- of female equality made her writings highly influential in the early women's movement.

(A) election
(B) advocacy
(C) neglect
(D) suspicion
(E) detection

2. The Mojave Desert's boundaries are generally ------- by the presence of Yucca brevifolia (Joshua trees), considered an indicator species for the region.

(A) integrated
(B) demarcated
(C) standardized
(D) challenged
(E) polarized

3. Even if the ------- in the authoritarian regime are sincere in their desire for democratic reform, they are unlikely to bring about immediate change.

(A) ambassadors
(B) dissidents
(C) loyalists
(D) denizens
(E) mercenaries

4. Not only are false memories common in normal life, but researchers have also found it easy to generate ------- recollections in the minds of laboratory subjects.

(A) inconsistent
(B) elaborate
(C) spurious
(D) diabolical
(E) cerebral

5. The notion that people who live alone are happier than those who do not is viewed with ------- because no known civilization has ------- solitary living as a social ideal.

(A) disbelief . . abhorred
(B) skepticism . . repudiated
(C) contemplation . . portended
(D) derision . . touted
(E) elation . . vaunted

6. The judge's -------, even foreboding appearance belied his ------- personality.

(A) eccentric . . glacial
(B) imposing . . condescending
(C) jovial . . mirthful
(D) austere . . ebullient
(E) grave . . authoritarian

Set 27 (Answers p. 124)

1. Noise from sonar can deafen sea creatures, but evidence suggests that whales can -------- the damage by blocking their ears.

    (A) lament
    (B) intensify
    (C) reveal
    (D) alleviate
    (E) reciprocate

2. Overdevelopment has led to the rapid -------- of the lake's crystal blue waters, a problem ------- by marine biologists during the environmental summit.

    (A) integration . . described
    (B) dilution . . acknowledged
    (C) degradation . . highlighted
    (D) restoration . . denounced
    (E) pollution . . denied

3. Certain musical styles have become so ------- that it is impossible for present-day composers not to be ------- by them.

    (A) popular . . moved
    (B) melodious . . deluded
    (C) outdated . . affected
    (D) cacophonous . . enervated
    (E) ubiquitous . . influenced

4. Before they ------- it in the 1780s, East India Company administrators generally ------- the practice of allowing employees to transport personal goods on company ships.

    (A) outlawed . . denounced
    (B) condoned . . allowed
    (C) prohibited . . sanctioned
    (D) discerned . . accepted
    (E) misplaced . . permitted

5. Many people suffer poor working conditions ------- because they fear that speaking out could cost them their jobs.

    (A) irrevocably
    (B) remotely
    (C) tacitly
    (D) vociferously
    (E) indignantly

6. Unlike Bram Stoker's other novels, which were written in a ------- fashion, *Dracula* was the product of a ------- effort, one that lasted seven years.

    (A) hasty . . verifiable
    (B) cursory . . protracted
    (C) slapdash . . haphazard
    (D) meticulous . . systematic
    (E) dexterous . . laborious

Set 28 (Answers p. 125)

1. Virtually all living creatures seek ------- in the form of unfamiliar smells, tastes, sights, sounds, and experiences.

    (A) repentance
    (B) modesty
    (C) novelty
    (D) solitude
    (E) curiosity

2. Nineteenth century "nature fakers" acquired their name by ------- details about animal behavior in order to portray the natural world in a sympathetic light.

    (A) describing
    (B) venerating
    (C) fabricating
    (D) tolerating
    (E) supplying

3. Greek myths were originally ------- through oral tradition; however, they are transmitted primarily in written form today.

(A) contained
(B) identified
(C) analyzed
(D) disseminated
(E) dispelled

4. While Diego Rivera was a bold optimist who ------- the glory of the Mexican Revolution, Clemente Orozco was more -------- about the consequences of the movement.

(A) perpetuated . . enthusiastic
(B) extolled . . apprehensive
(C) decried . . subdued
(D) stipulated . . anxious
(E) vituperated . . elated

5. After the introduction of the printing press, hand-illustrated parchment came to be viewed as -------, an outdated relic of a pre-technological age.

(A) an anachronism
(B) an omen
(C) a conversion
(D) an abatement
(E) a paradigm

6. Some crustaceans possess sensors so ------- that they can perceive minuscule distinctions between waves made by prey and those made by predators.

(A) lugubrious
(B) munificent
(C) prescient
(D) voluptuous
(E) discriminating

Set 29 (Answers p. 126)

1. Although there are over 800 languages native to Papua New Guinea, a small number have no more living speakers and are considered -------.

(A) colloquial
(B) exotic
(C) dialect
(D) extinct
(E) indigenous

2. Mozart was not only a composer but also -------: he was a pioneer in the business of concocting opera projects and promoting concerts of his works.

(A) an outcast
(B) a virtuoso
(C) an entrepreneur
(D) a prodigy
(E) an altruist

3. A source of dispute for decades, the linguist's theory has finally been ------- by compelling new evidence that appears to ------- it once and for all.

(A) renounced . . explain
(B) upheld . . initiate
(C) mitigated . . prove
(D) vindicated . . substantiate
(E) accepted . . circumvent

4. Different languages emphasize various facets of human experience, revealing notions of time, number, and color to be highly ------- rather than fixed and universal.

(A) elastic
(B) esoteric
(C) vivid
(D) immutable
(E) antiquated

5. Although Robert enjoyed painting, he was really a ------- who never took art seriously enough to pursue it as a career.

(A) prevaricator
(B) contemporary
(C) usurper
(D) aesthete
(E) dilettante

6. The author has been accused of writing novels that are both ------- and -------: not only are they excessively sentimental but they also lack psychological depth.

(A) maudlin . . profane
(B) cloying . . incidental
(C) bellicose . . shallow
(D) mawkish . . superficial
(E) erudite . . insipid

Set 30 (Answers p. 127)

1. Food production can be greatly ------- by techniques proven to help harvest rain and filter waste water to irrigate crops.

(A) disabled
(B) enhanced
(C) consumed
(D) fertilized
(E) marketed

2. Eva Peron was a well-known ------- who ------- countless hours as well as vast sums of money to combatting poverty and other social ills.

(A) altruist . . deported
(B) collaborator . . accumulated
(C) impersonator . . squandered
(D) philanthropist . . devoted
(E) traitor . . donated

3. Tumors in plants, unlike those in animals, are typically -------, causing little or no damage and rarely becoming invasive.

(A) innocuous
(B) organic
(C) aggressive
(D) invasive
(E) biological

4. Because Alison has a strong tendency to -------, her friends avoid asking her questions that require clear answers.

(A) rationalize
(B) dawdle
(C) acquiesce
(D) equivocate
(E) prevaricate

5. Despite his general air of -------, Sergey Lavrov is recognized as one of the most ------- diplomats in the world.

(A) equanimity . . eminent
(B) befuddlement . . astute
(C) geniality . . jovial
(D) skepticism . . magnanimous
(E) haplessness . . partisan

6. Shakespeare had ------- for ------- new words: more than 2,000 neologisms have been identified in his plays and poems.

(A) a justification . . theorizing
(B) a penchant . . impugning
(C) an abhorrence . . devising
(D) a propensity . . coining
(E) a disposition . . eschewing

Set 31 (Answers p. 128)

1. The stegosaurus is immediately ------- to dinosaur enthusiasts because of the ------- spikes and plates on its tail.

   (A) identifiable . . distinctive
   (B) interesting . . enervating
   (C) distasteful . . characteristic
   (D) striking . . assiduous
   (E) confined . . menacing

2. It is often helpful to read several books about the same topic, for each book will typically ------- aspects that the others -------.

   (A) express . . describe
   (B) alienate . . overlook
   (C) illuminate . . neglect
   (D) transcribe . . magnify
   (E) discuss . . defend

3. The reign of Shah Jahan is considered the Mughal Empire's golden age – the time when artistic production reached its -------.

   (A) abeyance
   (B) zenith
   (C) consensus
   (D) objective
   (E) conclusion

4. Jared had a habit of arguing unpopular positions, not so much because he agreed with them as because he reveled in -------.

   (A) contrarianism
   (B) adulation
   (C) pacifism
   (D) hubris
   (E) whimsy

5. Engineers suspected that the airplane's wings had ------- damage during the difficult landing but after thorough inspection concluded that they were in fact -------.

   (A) tolerated . . deficient
   (B) suspended . . intact
   (C) undergone . . treacherous
   (D) sustained . . sound
   (E) suffered . . resolute

6. Although she was at first -------, the senator slowly became more ------- as the interview progressed.

   (A) reticent . . loquacious
   (B) ostentatious . . candid
   (C) laconic . . diffident
   (D) garrulous . . impetuous
   (E) defensive . . obstreperous

Set 32 (Answers p. 129)

1. Recognizing the ------- of the developers' plan, the city council members ------- it.

   (A) efficiency . . denounced
   (B) consequences . . corrupted
   (C) benefits . . mocked
   (D) value . . questioned
   (E) inadequacy . . vetoed

2. Author and social activist Gloria Jean Watkins, who published her books under the name bell hooks, took her ------- from her grandmother, Bell Blair Hooks.

   (A) inspiration
   (B) perseverance
   (C) acclaim
   (D) pseudonym
   (E) anecdotes

3. Common wisdom holds that emotions ------- logical thinking; however, research indicates that an awareness of one's emotions can actually ------- the ability to reason clearly.

(A) impede . . enhance
(B) augment . . stimulate
(C) obstruct . . analyze
(D) inhibit . . hinder
(E) symbolize . . amplify

4. Employers who refuse to let their workers telecommute from home often argue that the lack of physical ------- makes it difficult to ------- the workers' productivity.

(A) reliance . . exacerbate
(B) experience . . gauge
(C) proximity . . ascertain
(D) dependency . . mitigate
(E) distance . . determine

5. Television writers enjoy including high-tech storylines because they know that most viewers have limited technological ------- and are thus unable to judge the ------- of the plots.

(A) intuition . . propriety
(B) acumen . . veracity
(C) susceptibility . . credibility
(D) inclination . . propensity
(E) expertise . . gravity

6. Alan Ginsberg's willingness to write about ------- subjects made him a ------- figure; in the 1950s, no reputable publishing company would even consider publishing "Howl."

(A) taboo . . polemical
(B) daunting . . canonical
(C) arcane . . controversial
(D) distasteful . . revered
(E) esoteric . . quixotic

Set 33 (Answers p. 130)

1. Martin is a ------- and ------- worker: he makes certain to finish each task completely and pays great attention to detail.

(A) superficial . . detached
(B) flexible . . ambitious
(C) thorough . . meticulous
(D) creative . . enthusiastic
(E) lackadaisical . . careful

2. Isamu Noguchi's sculptures are influenced by ------- styles and national traditions, including ones from the United States, Japan, France, Mexico, and China.

(A) contiguous
(B) accessible
(C) realistic
(D) appealing
(E) multifarious

3. Many primate species are terrestrial rather than -------, but all great apes possess adaptations for climbing trees.

(A) omnivorous
(B) arboreal
(C) predatory
(D) aquatic
(E) nomadic

4. The springtime blizzard was ------- occurrence: not for a century had a major snowstorm taken place in that season.

(A) an interminable
(B) an enthralling
(C) an imminent
(D) an exceptional
(E) a rousing

5. The brain receives around 30 representations of every image but ------- ninety percent of them, ------- only the information necessary to form a coherent whole.

(A) eliminates . . proliferating
(B) enhances . . reproducing
(C) invigorates . . corroborating
(D) winnows . . discarding
(E) eschews . . retaining

6. While medical training formally ------- the values of empathy and compassion, doctors say that the reality of practicing medicine more often encourages an attitude of -------.

(A) emancipates . . erudition
(B) eschews . . opprobrium
(C) advances . . apprehension
(D) espouses . . diffidence
(E) extols . . conjecture

Set 34 (Answers p. 131)

1. Alaskan Malamutes are sometimes mistaken for Siberian Huskies because the two dogs have similar appearances, but they actually exhibit a number of ------- traits.

(A) unexpected
(B) divergent
(C) striking
(D) aggressive
(E) common

2. Many attempts have been made to ------- the phylloxera louse, which has destroyed thousands of vineyards, but it has proven to be extremely ------- surviving.

(A) destroy . . resistant to
(B) amplify . . bewildered by
(C) eradicate . . adept at
(D) contain . . challenged by
(E) alleviate . . constrained by

3. Frida Kahlo's paintings are considered ------- because they blend elements of classic Mexican tradition with a variety of contemporary themes.

(A) syncretic
(B) recondite
(C) pedestrian
(D) invaluable
(E) objectionable

4. Reputable scholars do not ------- information that contradicts their own interpretations but rather ------- it, amending their ideas accordingly.

(A) deny . . annihilate
(B) publicize . . contemplate
(C) exonerate . . stifle
(D) suppress . . acknowledge
(E) ignore . . implicate

5. ------- that he had received insufficient ------- for his contributions to the company, Nikolai Tesla resigned from his job at Machine Works only six months after he arrived.

(A) Exultant . . plaudits
(B) Indignant . . accolades
(C) Repulsed . . exemptions
(D) Perplexed . . caveats
(E) Incensed . . demerits

6. Because her supervisor refused to ------- the exact reasons that her job had been eliminated, Shayla could only ------- the true motives behind her dismissal.

(A) enumerate . . surmise
(B) disclose . . determine
(C) elucidate . . substantiate
(D) exculpate . . alleviate
(E) peruse . . deduce

Set 35 (Answers p. 132)

1. Marc Chagall's paintings are full of -------, contrasting images placed next to one another with no apparent logic or reason.

   (A) juxtapositions
   (B) symbols
   (C) motifs
   (D) illustrations
   (E) representations

2. The taste receptors that line the tongue are not composed of a single protein but rather of several different proteins working in -------.

   (A) defense
   (B) reaction
   (C) vain
   (D) tandem
   (E) advance

3. Brazil's Carioca River was once so ------- for its pristine water that sailors stopped to ------- their water supplies at its mouth.

   (A) acclaimed . . discard
   (B) disdained . . amass
   (C) renowned . . replenish
   (D) reviled . . collect
   (E) marginalized . . consume

4. The discovery of the Shoemaker-Levy 9 comet was -------; it occurred purely by chance while its namesakes were searching for near-Earth objects.

   (A) infelicitous
   (B) chronological
   (C) specious
   (D) astronomical
   (E) serendipitous

5. Because researchers have discovered that an easily manufactured compound can ------- onset of the disease, they are ------- that new forms of treatment may soon be developed.

   (A) inhibit . . dubious
   (B) thwart . . bemused
   (C) arrest . . optimistic
   (D) permeate . . adamant
   (E) forestall . . incensed

6. The field of tap dance has seldom ------- astonishing solo dancers; it is exceptional tap choreographers that are rare.

   (A) scoffed at
   (B) wanted for
   (C) inquired about
   (D) tended toward
   (E) wavered about

Set 36 (Answers p. 134)

1. First planted in Virginia in 1609, rice has been ------- as a staple crop in the United States for over four centuries.

   (A) isolated
   (B) cultivated
   (C) retained
   (D) confiscated
   (E) multiplied

2. The Dutch provinces formed a loose confederation but maintained their -------, with each province appointing its own ruler and establishing its own laws.

   (A) humility
   (B) diligence
   (C) confidence
   (D) autonomy
   (E) revenue

3. Many beautiful artifacts were unearthed from the Roman villa in the twentieth century, but the process of ------- the structure actually began hundreds of years earlier.

    (A) excavating
    (B) stabilizing
    (C) defiling
    (D) registering
    (E) decorating

4. While several ancient Greek musical compositions have been preserved intact, most are now ------- and only hint at the melodies they contained.

    (A) fragmentary
    (B) unexceptional
    (C) consolidated
    (D) euphonious
    (E) despondent

5. The new anthology demonstrates that the author regards poetry not as a ------- his principle literary endeavor but rather as an ------- part of it.

    (A) negation of . . ephemeral
    (B) reaction to . . elemental
    (C) characteristic of . . acceptable
    (D) defense of . . illusory
    (E) diversion from . . integral

6. The Seri people have traditionally had no fixed settlements, choosing instead to maintain a ------- lifestyle.

    (A) cordial
    (B) sycophantic
    (C) peripatetic
    (D) dogmatic
    (E) duplicitous

7. While scientists do not believe that genetically engineering apples ------- people's safety, they do think it could ------- the fruit's image as a wholesome and natural food.

    (A) interrogates . . belie
    (B) compromises . . undermine
    (C) reduces . . admonish
    (D) reinforces . . bolster
    (E) jeopardizes . . dominate

8. The notion that authors should write about what they know is often scorned for leading to the kind of literary ------- that many novels and memoirs do in fact exhibit.

    (A) pedantry
    (B) sophistry
    (C) obfuscation
    (D) profundity
    (E) solipsism

Set 37 (Answers p. 135)

1. *A People's History of the United States* is considered ------- work because it was the first book to present American history through the eyes of the common people.

    (A) an eloquent
    (B) a groundbreaking
    (C) a controversial
    (D) a meticulous
    (E) a comprehensive

2. The Iroquois belts called wampum served a ------- as well as -------- function: the beaded designs chronicled tribal legends and served as a medium for exchanging goods.

    (A) practical . . an abstract
    (B) literary . . an economic
    (C) social . . an individual
    (D) interpretive . . a cautionary
    (E) military . . a cohesive

3. In the age of Shakespeare and Milton, paper was -------: a few lines of print could be blotted out, but producing draft after draft was prohibitively expensive.

   (A) a concession
   (B) an implement
   (C) a luxury
   (D) an innovation
   (E) a commodity

4. In the moments before the press conference began, the mayor ------- with reporters, making small talk and cracking jokes.

   (A) bantered
   (B) commiserated
   (C) sauntered
   (D) circulated
   (E) indulged

5. Because infrared light cannot currently be used by solar panels, a cell that could harvest such light would be a ------- for the sustainable energy industry.

   (A) harbinger
   (B) rationale
   (C) boon
   (D) dichotomy
   (E) regression

6. Although William tried to ------- his friend after their argument, his attempts were futile; in fact, they only ------- her irritation.

   (A) placate . . mitigated
   (B) conjure . . compounded
   (C) pacify . . curtailed
   (D) castigate . . augmented
   (E) mollify . . exacerbated

7. Crucial to the internationalization of science has been the emergence of English as the undisputed world language, but this linguistic ------- presents challenges for both native and non-native speakers.

   (A) ambivalence
   (B) dichotomy
   (C) diatribe
   (D) hegemony
   (E) vernacular

8. The detectives were unable to comprehend the suspect's motives, which, to their chagrin, remained frustratingly -------.

   (A) impenitent
   (B) recondite
   (C) candid
   (D) deviant
   (E) opaque

Set 38 (Answers p. 136)

1. The movie's plot initially seemed -------, but a series of unexpected plot twists made the ending impossible to -------.

   (A) trite . . evoke
   (B) entertaining . . imagine
   (C) confusing . . comprehend
   (D) predictable . . foresee
   (E) amusing . . ignore

2. The grapefruit is ------- fruit: it results from a cross between the Jamaican sweet orange and the Asian pomelo.

   (A) a hybrid
   (B) a temperate
   (C) a ubiquitous
   (D) a culinary
   (E) an exotic

3. Part of Joseph Epstein's appeal as a writer is his willingness to say precisely what he thinks, even at the risk of ------- his friends and acquaintances.

(A) antagonizing
(B) mollifying
(C) satirizing
(D) selecting
(E) impressing

4. The intensity of Beethoven's *Eroica* symphony makes hearing it a ------- experience, one that leaves listeners utterly drained of emotion.

(A) tedious
(B) bombastic
(C) cathartic
(D) ineffable
(E) clandestine

5. Although Peter Abelard was expected to pursue a military career, he ------- that option, choosing to study philosophy instead.

(A) contemplated
(B) stipulated
(C) eschewed
(D) deferred
(E) commended

6. *Commedia dell'arte* is known for its -------- acting style, which emphasizes exaggerated gestures and unrestrained shows of emotion.

(A) authentic
(B) ironic
(C) credible
(D) histrionic
(E) cloying

7. Despite the tendency to see Baroque architecture as an exclusively European phenomenon, it not only ------- but was also inextricably ------- to the rise of colonialism.

(A) coincided with . . linked
(B) relied on . . inured
(C) deviated from . . bound
(D) borrowed from . . attracted
(E) railed against . . partial

8. The author is rarely explicit about stating his -------, a strategy that ------- any understanding of what he truly believes.

(A) allegations . . reiterates
(B) prerogatives . . inhibits
(C) convictions . . forestalls
(D) proclivities . . belies
(E) incentives . . precludes

Set 39 (Answers p. 138)

1. Astronomy is not to be confused with astrology: although the two fields share a common origin they are now entirely -------.

(A) contrived
(B) theoretical
(C) incomprehensible
(D) distinct
(E) established

2. With about 1,200 known species, the skinks (scincidae) are the second most ------- family of lizards, exceeded only by the geckos.

(A) territorial
(B) diverse
(C) fascinating
(D) dangerous
(E) exotic

3. Some proponents of string theory have become so ------- the ideals of "elegance" and "symmetry" that they are unable to acknowledge its flaws.

    (A) perplexed by
    (B) disturbed by
    (C) accustomed to
    (D) opposed to
    (E) enamored with

4. As agricultural societies grew in complexity during the Neolithic periods, rivalries within groups had to be ------- so that the larger collective could flourish.

    (A) emboldened
    (B) displayed
    (C) chastised
    (D) anticipated
    (E) quelled

5. The first phone booths were ------- of craftsmanship; they were not simply convenient places to have a conversation but works of art in their own right.

    (A) compilations
    (B) forerunners
    (C) amalgams
    (D) attributes
    (E) paragons

6. The critic's position on some works is disappointingly -------, but his analysis of other works is, in contrast, surprisingly ------- and penetrating.

    (A) seductive . . flippant
    (B) pedestrian . . lucid
    (C) convoluted . . nebulous
    (D) vapid . . insipid
    (E) astute . . insightful

7. The professor's enthusiasm was -------: even students with no prior interest in the subject found that their interest was piqued.

    (A) evanescent
    (B) gratuitous
    (C) infectious
    (D) seditious
    (E) intractable

8. The government's policy of fiscal ------- is increasingly ------- to voters, who resent the elimination of services that they have come to take for granted.

    (A) oscillation . . expendable
    (B) augmentation . . inimical
    (C) inflation . . adaptable
    (D) indulgence . . patronizing
    (E) austerity . . objectionable

Set 40 (Answers p. 139)

1. Bison were once hunted to near extinction, but they have experienced a ------- because of conservation efforts and commercial demand.

    (A) collapse
    (B) modification
    (C) resurgence
    (D) detection
    (E) reluctance

2. Valentina Tereshkova was not only the first woman to fly into space but she was also the first ------- : all of the previous astronauts had served in the military.

    (A) commander
    (B) itinerant
    (C) mediator
    (D) ingenue
    (E) civilian

3. Unlike most capital cities, Suva did not grow up around a single industry but gradually developed by attracting workers in a ------- of fields.

(A) plethora
(B) derivation
(C) recapitulation
(D) sequence
(E) scarcity

4. Like his grandfather, James Joyce, Steven Joyce is intensely suspicious of biographers and frequently attempts to ------- their efforts to write about his famous ancestor's life.

(A) augment
(B) engage
(C) thwart
(D) contemplate
(E) peruse

5. Artificial intelligence began with the goal of ------- machines with the ------- of reason and creativity as well as the capacity to learn from experience.

(A) exculpating . . capacities
(B) creating . . detriments
(C) endowing . . faculties
(D) winnowing . . perceptions
(E) articulating . . enigmas

6. Despite a widespread tendency to ------- his poor health, many modern critics argue that Vincent van Gogh was deeply frustrated by the inactivity brought on by his bouts of illness.

(A) excoriate
(B) palliate
(C) invigorate
(D) romanticize
(E) illustrate

7. Long ------- as a ------- for numerous ills, aloe vera has been used in herbal medicine since the first century AD.

(A) scrutinized . . virtue
(B) harangued . . cure
(C) touted . . panacea
(D) praised . . deficiency
(E) jettisoned . . therapy

8. Augusta King was -------, foreseeing that computers could carry out complex operations nearly a century before they were invented.

(A) prescient
(B) irreverent
(C) enervating
(D) obdurate
(E) beguiling

Set 41 (Answers p. 140)

1. The company's effort to ship more cargo by rail received help from a source so ------- that no one outside the transport sector initially noticed it.

(A) obscure
(B) extensive
(C) distinguished
(D) optimistic
(E) deft

2. Although archaeologists have made many attempts to ------- the ancient cuneiform writing, they continue to be ------- by its meaning.

(A) display . . enervated
(B) evade . . stymied
(C) excavate . . garbled
(D) determine . . elated
(E) decipher . . confounded

3. Because the author's will included ------- prohibiting the distribution of her letters, they have never been published in their entirety.

(A) an anthology
(B) a eulogy
(C) a tome
(D) an embargo
(E) an abridgement

4. The Internet has transformed the illegal distribution of copyrighted material from an activity that is merely difficult to -------- to one that is virtually impossible to -------.

(A) enable . . deter
(B) prosecute . . recommend
(C) denounce . . replicate
(D) prevent . . encourage
(E) restrict . . contain

5. Although George wanted to be seen as detached and -------, he actually cared deeply about what people thought of him.

(A) obstinate
(B) aloof
(C) charismatic
(D) infallible
(E) sycophantic

6. Hesiod's "Works and Days" is ------- poem, one that employs mythological examples to instruct its readers in how to lead a successful life.

(A) a loquacious
(B) an ambiguous
(C) a didactic
(D) a droll
(E) a vivid

7. Although the actress was once praised for her nuanced and passionate characterizations, her most recent performances have been ------- and oddly devoid of -------.

(A) ebullient . . enthusiasm
(B) half-hearted . . belligerence
(C) subtle . . imagination
(D) predictable . . sonority
(E) generic . . conviction

8. In his paintings, Edvard Munch ------- outside influences with his own original visions, blurring the line between originality and -------.

(A) combined . . verisimilitude
(B) complemented . . profundity
(C) elucidated . . candor
(D) blended . . iconoclasm
(E) synthesized . . mimesis

Set 42 (Answers p. 142)

1. Winston Churchill's writings were a ------- part of his politics because they introduced his ideas to a wide audience and made him a household name.

(A) legible
(B) discerning
(C) courageous
(D) significant
(E) deleterious

2. The producers of Sesame Street have developed a ------- model of television production, one that ------- interaction between producers, writers, and educators.

(A) an elaborate . . exemplifies
(B) an innovative . . attenuates
(C) a defensive . . encourages
(D) a communal . . dissuades
(E) a collaborative . . emphasizes

3. After the newspaper's headquarters were

partially destroyed by fire, reporters continued to work there until authorities ------- the building.

(A) vanquished
(B) surveyed
(C) commandeered
(D) ascertained
(E) investigated

4. Like many of his characters, Dickens was raised in -------: he was forced to leave school to work in a factory after his father was thrown into debtors' prison.

(A) penury
(B) solitude
(C) temperance
(D) penitence
(E) affluence

5. A new method of applying coatings to microscopic objects has ------- a process that was traditionally time-consuming and -------.

(A) expedited . . indecorous
(B) facilitated . . minimalistic
(C) extracted . . interminable
(D) associated . . unwieldy
(E) streamlined . . convoluted

6. Many commentators argued that the classical music festival could be ------- only if it were completely reinvented, yet its recent success has demonstrated the effectiveness of a less ------- approach.

(A) enhanced . . formulaic
(B) rescued . . innocuous
(C) expanded . . contemporary
(D) salvaged . . radical
(E) promoted . . partisan

7. Although heavy storms often ------- the

island with heavy rains and high winds, they tend to be ephemeral, ------- after about an hour.

(A) pummel . . intensifying
(B) bypass . . disappearing
(C) blanket . . dissipating
(D) transgress . . evaporating
(E) drench . . converging

8. Although the author's style is occasionally heavy-handed and lacking in --------, that deficiency does not ------- the importance of the questions he asks.

(A) subtlety . . legitimize
(B) significance . . clarify
(C) nuance . . trivialize
(D) aplomb . . dignify
(E) ineptitude . . portend

Set 43 (Answers p. 143)

1. Economist Jeffrey Sachs was -------- scholar, beginning college-level mathematics at the age of only thirteen.

(A) a meticulous
(B) an inquisitive
(C) a precocious
(D) a versatile
(E) a literate

2. Arsenic is a -------- substance whose ------- of groundwater is a problem that afflicts millions of people worldwide.

(A) complex . . anticipation
(B) toxic . . contamination
(C) flimsy . . deprivation
(D) destructive . . purification
(E) buoyant . . pollution

3. Scientists who receive too many ------- often

develop an arrogance that prevents them from perceiving the kinds of ------- solutions that led to their original success.

(A) demonstrations . . remarkable
(B) kudos . . baseless
(C) hypotheses . . ingenious
(D) critiques . . creative
(E) accolades . . novel

4. When Queen Victoria ascended the throne, the powers of the British sovereign had been sharply -------; nevertheless, she ------- an influence over government policy throughout her reign.

(A) controlled . . impeded
(B) exacerbated . . demonstrated
(C) curtailed . . exerted
(D) assuaged . . declaimed
(E) reduced . . prompted

5. Unlike sheep, which are ------- and obedient animals, kangaroos are ------- and poorly suited to life on a ranch.

(A) timorous . . recalcitrant
(B) obstinate . . wily
(C) docile . . indulgent
(D) intrepid . . litigious
(E) apathetic . . apprehensive

6. Before the construction of the Berlin Wall, more than three million East Germans ------- emigration restrictions and crossed over the border into West Berlin.

(A) circumvented
(B) admonished
(C) lauded
(D) debunked
(E) expedited

7. Louis XIV of France (1638-1715) demanded

that his courtiers behave in ------- manner, rewarding those whose were most -------.

(A) a decorous . . assiduous
(B) a capricious . . ingratiating
(C) a sycophantic . . obsequious
(D) an abstemious . . effusive
(E) an incorrigible . . solicitous

8. Ed Ruscha's artwork is strongly influenced by the movie industry: his *Mountain Series* evokes a film studio logo, and *Large Trademark with Eight Spotlights* (1962) is ------- of a movie screen.

(A) reverent
(B) redolent
(C) defiant
(D) contemplative
(E) exploitive

Set 44 (Answers p. 145)

1. Known for their ------- temperaments, Yorkshire Terriers are typically gentle and easy to train.

(A) impulsive
(B) vivacious
(C) obedient
(D) morose
(E) shrewd

2. Confrontations between protestors and government officials have ------- in recent weeks, with both sides showing a staunch unwillingness to -------.

(A) intensified . . offend
(B) dwindled . . compromise
(C) vacillated . . improvise
(D) escalated . . negotiate
(E) increased . . persist

3. The results of the researcher's experiment

were so astounding that their implications could hardly be -------.

(A) denied
(B) announced
(C) protected
(D) substantiated
(E) conceived

4. Lonesome George, the last surviving Pinta tortoise, became ------- for conservation-minded tourists, thousands of whom ------ for a glimpse of him each year.

(A) an activist . . surrendered
(B) an icon . . clamored
(C) a beacon . . foundered
(D) an epistle . . competed
(E) a paradigm. . compromised

5. Many observers have attempted to detect tension between Angela Merkel and her main rival, Peer Steinbrück, but their public relationship has remained -------

(A) scandalous
(B) precarious
(C) fractious
(D) acerbic
(E) amicable

6. Voters who hoped that the new government would prove more -------- than the previous one were disappointed to discover that it was just as -------, its promises just as vague.

(A) flexible . . manipulative
(B) judicious . . bureaucratic
(C) transparent . . calculating
(D) lucrative . . corrupt
(E) decisive . . equivocal

7. Any type of design that is sufficiently

attractive to achieve widespread popularity risks turning into a cliché, but some designs succeed in becoming ------- without seeming -------.

(A) conventional . . banal
(B) acceptable . . ludicrous
(C) ubiquitous . . trite
(D) enfranchised. . coercive
(E) understated . . hackneyed

8. The essay is considered a ------- genre because of the ease with which it shifts to accommodate authors' individual styles.

(A) pedantic
(B) decadent
(C) munificent
(D) protean
(E) soporific

Set 45 (Answers p. 146)

1. Aung San Suu Kyi has spent much of her life in seclusion, yet she is of the most ------- political figures of the twenty-first century.

(A) energetic
(B) permanent
(C) recognizable
(D) sympathetic
(E) neglected

2. Henry David Thoreau is sometimes viewed as -------, although his writings seem to call for improving rather than abolishing government.

(A) a democrat
(B) an anarchist
(C) an oligarch
(D) a conservative
(E) a pragmatist

3. The D'Oyly Carte opera company kept

Gilbert and Sullivan's operettas in the public eye for over a century, leaving ------- legacy of production styles that continues to be ------- in new performances.

(A) an enduring . . emulated
(B) a potent . . resisted
(C) an eclectic . . censored
(D) a permanent . . defied
(E) an idealized. . reflected

4. Brewed by forcing a small quantity of pressurized boiling water through finely ground coffee beans, espresso is so ------- that it almost has the consistency of syrup.

(A) translucent
(B) aromatic
(C) viscous
(D) potent
(E) amorphous

5. *The Rite of Spring*, which ------- a riot during its premiere, was largely responsible for establishing Stravinsky's reputation as ------- who pushed the boundaries of musical design.

(A) provoked . . an iconoclast
(B) placated . . a recidivist
(C) enumerated . . a lackey
(D) disturbed . . an innovator
(E) inspired . . a charlatan

6. Contemporary historians of science have a tendency to ------- the originality of the so-called scientific revolution, and to stress instead its ------- with medieval alchemy.

(A) downplay . . frustration
(B) deprecate . . continuity
(C) explain . . convergence
(D) trivialize . . rupture
(E) promote . . concurrence

7. Although the book is ambitious in scope, it fails to offer a ------- argument but rather presents a ------- collection of testimonies interspersed with the author's commentary.

(A) pervasive . . facetious
(B) disparate . . quixotic
(C) cohesive . . motley
(D) scholarly . . studious
(E) comprehensive . . definitive

8. Mountain weather is infamously -------: cloudless skies can abruptly give way to torrential rains or even heavy snows.

(A) mercurial
(B) effusive
(C) obstreperous
(D) temperate
(E) anomalous

Answer Key and Explanations

Exercise: Breaking it Down (p. 33)

1. B

The word "rigid" is a key word for this question; it lets you know that the blank will mean something similar to rigid. The second half of the sentence tells you that in contrast to the human figures, animals are lifelike: in other words, the human figures are NOT lifelike. Thus, for the blank, you want a negative word that means "rigid" or "not lifelike." "Dazzling," "revolutionary," "satirical," and "realistic" don't mean "not lifelike," so eliminate them. "Realistic" might be tempting, but remember: you want a word that means the opposite of "lifelike," not the same thing. "Artificial" is the only word that fits, so (B) is correct.

2. A

In this sentence, the word "belies" signals a contradiction, letting you know that the outer appearance will somehow form a contrast to the "fiery pools of lava." Good words to fill in the blank here might include "peaceful" or "safe." Choice (A) is the only answer that logically contrasts with fiery pools of lava (placid means "peaceful;" think of the root PLAC-, meaning "peace"), so (A) is the right answer. "Cavernous" might seem to fit because it logically fits with underground pools of lava, but remember that you want a contrasting word for the blank. "Noxious," "belligerent," and "ludicrous" don't mean "peaceful," so cross them off. Even if you aren't sure about "noxious" and "belligerent," you can use the roots NOC/NOX- (harm) and BELL- (war), to figure out that they're both negative.

3. C

The sentence tells you that his early drawings are "well-done and expressive," but they don't quite reach the "level of _____" of his "most celebrated" works. This lets you know that the second blank will be a better or more emphatic version of "well-done and expressive." For your own word, try filling in "genius" or something similar. "Mediocrity" and "instability" are negative, so eliminate them. Even if you don't know what "mediocrity" means, look for the root MED-, which has to do with the middle: something in the middle isn't likely to be outstanding or genius. "Serenity" and "efficiency" are positive, but neither one of them is a stronger way of describing something "well-done and expressive." Answer choice (C) is correct because "virtuosity" means "genius."

4. C

"Compete with one another" is a key phrase in this sentence; it tells you that word in the blank will be something positive (something that the sisters want to compete for). "Hierarchy" lets you know that the word will have something to do with status or power, because a hierarchy is a way of ranking individuals according to authority or superiority. "Relative" seems to fit with "position" at first, but remember that you want a word describing a good kind of position; "relative" only means "in relation to something else," so it could be good or bad. Thus, you can cross off "relative," "cumbersome," "surreptitious," and "peripheral" because these words all have negative or neutral connotations. Even if you aren't sure what "peripheral" means, you can use the root word PERI- (around) to help you: you want a word that means "on top," not "around the outside." The only answer choice left with a strong positive connotation is "dominant," and since "dominant" also refers to superiority and power, (C) is the correct answer.

5. E

Key words in the first part of the sentence include "essential role" and "effective." These positive qualities are the reasons why scientists are doubting the characterization of music "as _____." Therefore, you know that the word in the blank must be negative and mean the opposite of "essential" or "effective." "Useless" or "silly" might be good words to fill in the blank. "Aesthetic" (related to beauty) might be tempting, but it doesn't fit in the context of the sentence. "Invigorating" is also tempting, because it means almost the same thing as "more effective than speech at improving people's moods," but remember that you want a word that means the opposite of this. "Mellifluous" is positive (think of the same root in "melody"), so you can cross off (B). "Demanding" is negative, but doesn't mean "useless." "Frivolous" means "having no practical purpose," so (E) is correct.

6. B

The key word "paradoxically" tells you that the two parts of the sentence will contrast with each other. So, since "creative success" in the first part is a positive idea, it will require something negative in the second part. "Stipulation," "embellishment," "repetition," and "dissemination" of a cherished ideal aren't negative. If you aren't sure what "dissemination" means, note the roots DIS- (apart) and SEM- (seed): to disseminate is to spread something around. The "renunciation" (giving up – notice the prefix RE-, "back") of something precious is negative, so (B) is correct.

7. B

The key word in this sentence is "earliest known;" this clues you in that you could fill in "an early form" or something similar for the blank. (A) and (E) are both trap answers because they give you the opposite of what you want: the modern-day camera is a "descendant" or an "heir" of the camera obscura, not the other way around. A "relic" is a leftover, so (C) is also backwards. "Proponent" makes no sense: look at the root words PRO- (supporting) and PON- (put): a proponent is a supporter. Since "forerunner" means "early form," choice (B) is the right answer.

8. B

The key phrase here is "from weighty ledgers to nautical maps." Even if you aren't sure exactly what a ledger is, the construction "from…to" lets you know that you're looking for a word describing many different kinds of physical things. "Diatribes" (rants), "caveats" (warnings), "foibles" (faults), and "euphemisms" (nicer ways of saying unpleasant things – note the root EU-, "good" or "well") aren't physical things that you could show off in an exhibition. The only word that fits in the blank is (B), paraphernalia.

9. D

The key words are "from the earliest years of his childhood," so you want a word in the blank that refers to a very young age. "Cursory" (brief) "trivial" (unimportant) "hackneyed" (unoriginal) and "circumspect" (cautious) don't have anything to do with a young age. For "circumspect," note the roots word CIRCUM- (around) and SPEC- (look at), which can give you a clue that this isn't the word you want. "Precocious" means "starting unusually young" (the root PRE-, "before," will give you a clue about this even if you aren't sure what "precocious" means), so the answer is (D).

10. C

A key word here is "promises." The question specifies that because the leaders have trouble keeping their promises, they'll also have trouble meeting the "_____ set out…in the new contract." You know that the word in the blank will be something that could logically be set out in a contract, and something similar to promises. A good word for the blank might be "agreements" or "rules." For "innovations," look at the root word NOV- (new): an innovation is a new invention, which doesn't make sense as a synonym for "promises." "Quandaries," "enigmas," and "dichotomies" also don't fit. Since "stipulations" means "terms" or "rules," (C) is correct.

11. C

The key word is "questioned" – the word in the first blank must refer to a person who questions something. A "partisan" is someone with a strong bias toward one side or another, so (A) doesn't fit. "Detractors" (note the prefix DE-) are people who argue against something. "Naysayers" literally means "people who say nay (no)," so this doesn't fit either. A zealot is someone who is unreasonably enthusiastic about a cause, so this is definitely the wrong choice. "Skeptics" are people who question what they're told, so (C) makes sense for the first blank. For "proffering," look at the root word PRO- (forward) + "offering:" this word means "putting forward for consideration," which makes sense in the second blank, so (C) is correct.

12. A

Start with the second blank because you have a stronger clue word: "independent and neutral." You want "less _____" to mean "independent and neutral," so the blank will mean the opposite. "Erudite" (wise) and "adept" (skillful) don't fit. "Disinterested" (objective) is clearly wrong. Both "partisan" and "litigious" might work in the second blank, so check the first blank to see which one is correct. For the first blank, you could fill in your own word – "process" or "way" might be good choices. "Paradigm" fits, but "consensus" means agreement (note the root word CON-, meaning "together"), which doesn't make sense. Thus, (A) is correct.

13. D

Start with the second blank. The clue for the second blank is "from which it cannot recover," so you know you want a negative word that means something like "be damaged." To "evolve" is to change in a good way, so this doesn't make sense. The clue actually says "cannot recover," so "recover" is clearly wrong. Looking at "forestall," note the root FORE- (before): this word means to stop something

before it starts. That doesn't mean "be damaged," so cross it off. To "crest" is to reach the top of something, which is the opposite of the word you want. Thus, even if you aren't sure what "deteriorate" means, it's the only answer choice left. The negative prefix DE- should give you a hint; this word means "become worse" or "become damaged." "Thrive" (be healthy) fits in the first blank, so (D) is correct.

14. E

For the first blank, the clue word "respected" lets you know that you need a positive word. "Scrupulous" is the only word in the list with a positive connotation. For the second blank, you want a word that gives the relationship between evidence and facts: a good word to fill in might be "prove" or "show." "Mock" is clearly wrong. "Determine" and "dictate" could both work for this blank, but (B) is wrong because "capricious" (changing one's mind often) doesn't work for the first blank. Thus, (E) is correct.

Easy (p. 37)

1. D

Make sure to follow the key words in the sentence instead of getting waylaid by things that are true about Queen Elizabeth but not good fits for the clues. The key phrase – the information after the colon – talks about how many languages she spoke, so don't get tempted by "monarchist" or "sovereign;" they might describe a queen, but they have nothing to do with languages. A patron is someone who supports something else, also irrelevant. For misanthrope, break the word down into MIS-, against, and ANTHRO-, human being: this word describes someone who hates other people, so eliminate (C) as well. In (D), the root POLY-, many, gives you a clue: a polyglot is someone who speaks many different languages, so (D) is correct. Connecting the idea of speaking many languages to the root POLY- allows you to spot the probable answer almost immediately.

2. B

The key words "higher quality" indicate that the hand-printed books were viewed positively. The sentence contrasts them with the inexpensive printed books, which must therefore be negative. So to describe the inexpensive books, you want a negative word that has something to do with lower quality. "Criticized" or "disliked" might be good options to fill in the blank. "Disparaged" (note the negative prefix DIS-) means "criticized," so (B) is correct. "Recommended, "salvaged" (saved), "embellished" (beautified), and "accumulated" are all positive and do not fit the clue.

3. B

The information that the cheetah population has changed from 100,000 to 10,000 tells you that the word in the blank must mean something like "dropped." That is the definition of "plummeted," so (B) is correct. "Migrated" (moved from one area to another), "capitulated" (gave in), and "defected" (deserted one's country) all do not make sense. In (E), "proliferated" (grew, spread) is the opposite of what you're looking for.

4. A

The list "levitation," "flight," and "ESP" tell you that you're looking for a word that means "supernatural." That is the definition of "fantastical," so (A) is correct. "Nefarious" (evil, NE-, not + FAR-, do), "creative," "unpredictable," and "delusional" (false belief) all do not fit.

5. C

The second half of the sentence tells you what you need for the blank: Weil felt bad for the soldiers who had no sugar, so she refused to eat any either. Try filling in "caring about others" or something similar in the blank. "Empathy" means "identifying with others' feelings," so (C) is correct. "Erudition" (deep knowledge) is associated with philosophers, but that's not what

the clue says, so eliminate it. "Objectivity" (not being influenced by emotion) is really the opposite of what you want, so eliminate (B). "Contempt" (disdain) is exactly the opposite of what you're looking for, and "sophistry" (making false arguments) does not make sense, so eliminate (D) and (E).

6. B

This question looks somewhat more difficult than it actually is. The key words "criticized" and "contaminating" tell you that the word in the blank will be negative and refer to someone opposed to fracking. (B) is the only negative answer (look at the prefix DE-, not), and it is the only word consistent with the clue. (A) and (C) are clearly positive (look at BENE-, good in "benefactor). "Acolytes" (followers) does not fit, as is true for "solicitors" (a person who tries to create business). Remember that it does not matter whether you know (D) and (E), as long as you can recognize that "detractor" fits.

7. E

The information after the colon emphasizes that the python eats many different kinds of things. Try plugging in a word like "varied" or "diverse." That is the definition of "heterogeneous" (HETERO-, different), so (E) is correct. "Salutary" (healthy), "restricted," and "exclusive" clearly don't make sense. Careful with (C): although "naturalistic" looks like "natural," and the sentence does indicate that the python eats things found in nature, the word actually means "*imitating* nature" (e.g. a naturalistic painting) and, furthermore, does not fit with the idea of eating lots of different kinds of things.

8. E

The key word "while" tells you that the two blanks will have opposite meanings. In addition, the phrase "*too much* physical exertion" tells you that the second blank will be negative. Start with the second side. You can eliminate (B) and (D) since "salutary" means "healthy" and "pervasive" means "present everywhere." Now look at the first side. Since it's the opposite of the second, you know the word must be positive. "Detrimental" and "dangerous" are both negative, so eliminate (A) and (C). That leaves (E): "beneficial" means "good" (BENE-, good), and "deleterious" means "bad" (think of "delete"), so both words fit.

9. C

The information after the semicolon tells you that the correct answer will be related to the idea that *no* ice skater had *ever* received such extensive media coverage. "Unprecedented" fits because it means "never been done before" (UN-, not + PRE-, before). "Inexplicable" (mysterious), "trivial" (unimportant), "unsustainable" (unable to be maintained), and "recurrent" (happening over and over again) all do not fit.

10. E

Look at the information after the colon for clues to the sentence. The sentence contrasts the high, snowy forest rim, with the low, warm areas. In other words, the weather changes (fluctuates) according to how high or low the landscape is (its elevation). So the answer is (E). For the first side, you can cross off (B) and (D) because "accelerates" (goes faster) does not make sense, and "stabilizes" is the opposite of what you're looking for. For the second side, you can eliminate (A) because "climate" has nothing to do with how high or low something is. It's also a synonym for "weather," and it makes no sense to say "weather changes according to weather." In (C), "wilderness" also has nothing to nothing to do with being high or low, so that leaves (E), which fits.

11. B

The key phrase "rally for its restoration" gives you a clue about the first blank: things only need to be restored when they're in poor condition, so you know you're looking for a negative word that means something like "falling apart." That is the definition of "decrepitude," so (B) is

correct. "Urbanity" (sophistication) is positive, so eliminate (A). "Vigor" (energy, health) is positive, so eliminate (C). "Compunction" (guilt) is negative but makes no sense in context, so eliminate (D). And "density" (number of people living in a given area) is neutral and does not fit the sentence, so eliminate (E).

12. D

Why would suppressing (not allowing) low-level forest fires inevitably lead to more dangerous fires? Because those low-level fires would destroy materials that burn easily. So the first blank must have something to do with burning easily.

If there were no fires to destroy the materials, however, then the materials would increase. So the second blank must mean something like "increase."

Start with the second blank since it's a little more straightforward. "Dissipate" (disappear), "demolish" (destroy), and "entangle" (get tangled up in) all don't fit, so eliminate (A), (C), and (E). Now look at the first blank: it must refer to materials that burn easily – something like "flammable." "Insoluble" means "unable to dissolve," which doesn't fit (something that doesn't dissolve doesn't necessarily burn easily), so eliminate (B). "Combustible" means "explosive" or "prone to going up in flames," so (D) is correct.

13. E

If the population soared, you can assume that the immigrants were entering Philadelphia, so you want a word that describes a large migration. In (E), look at the roots IN + FLUX-, flow: an influx is a movement towards or into a place, so (E) is correct. A diminution (look at the root word MIN-, small, as in miniature) is a decrease, which is exactly the opposite of what you want. "Consensus" (agreement), "evacuation," and "abeyance" (stopping) do not fit.

14. D

The word in the blank is contrasted with "from a playful *distance*," so you're looking for a word that means the opposite of "distance." "Immerses" means "surrounds completely," so (D) is correct. "Harmonizes" is related to music but not to the sentence, and "identifies," "complements" (completes or improves), and "validates" (proves) all do not fit.

15. C

Since the administrators were found to have authorized the purchase of stolen items, you can assume the foreign officials weren't too happy. So you're looking for a negative word that means something like "criticized." "Rebuked" means "strongly criticized," so (C) fits. "Mollified" (soothed) and "esteemed" (held in high regard) are positive, so eliminate (A) and (B). Careful with (D): the people who rebuked the administrators would likely be exasperated (extremely annoyed), not the other way around. "Desecrated" (destroyed something holy) just doesn't make sense, so (E) can be eliminated as well.

16. C

Try to fill in your own word for the blank: puns are used to make fun of people or things, and logically, they must have been acceptable because they were viewed as positive. But careful with the negation: the fact that puns did something "*without* _____ the established social order" indicates that you're looking for a negative word. So "threatening" or "damaging" would be good choices for the blank. "Undermining" means "overturning or destroying in an underhanded way," so (C) is correct. "Improving" is exactly the opposite of the word you want. "Stabilizing" and "unifying" are also contrary to the idea of threatening, so (D) and (E) can be eliminated. "Constructing" makes no sense in context," so (B) can be eliminated as well.

17. B

The key phrase "in order to limit the influence of any single region" tells you that the word in the blank must mean something like "spread around." That is the definition of "disperse," so (B) is correct. "Legislate" means "enacting laws" – it has nothing to do with spreading power around, so eliminate (A). "Justify" and "exploit" (take advantage of) both do not make sense in context, so eliminate (C) and (D). Careful with (E): a government "demonstrating" power isn't the same thing as spreading power around. In the former case, all the power can still come from one place; in the latter, power has to come from lots of different places.

18. B

The sentence sets up a contrast between the blank and the fact that George Washington Carver is *believed* to have been born in January of 1864, so plug in something like "unknown." The word closest in meaning is "speculative" (subject to guesswork), so (B) is correct. "Evident" is the opposite of what you're looking for, so eliminate (A). "Celebratory" and "annual" are both related to birthdays, but neither fits the sentence, so eliminate (C) and (E). "Unattainable" simply does not make sense, so (D) can be eliminated as well.

19. E

The key word "defeat" tells you that the first blank is negative, and the key phrase "falling under foreign rule" tells you that the second blank must also be negative and mean "independence." That should lead you directly to (B) and (E); "rivalry," "uniqueness," and "cosmopolitanism" (sophistication) do not make sense. (B) cannot work because "thrived" (flourished) is positive, but in (E), "declined" fits for the first blank.

20. A

The key phrases "long been a mystery" and "soon be resolved" tell you that the word in the blank must be a synonym for "mystery." The only word that fits that definition is "enigma," so (A) is correct. "Dichotomy" (paradox, apparent contradiction), "tradition," "aptitude" (ability), and "fallacy" (error) all do not fit.

Medium (p. 39)

1. A

The information after the colon defines the blank – the word must mean, "showing no reaction to pain or physical discomfort." That is the definition of "stoicism," so (A) is correct. "Impetuousness" (impulsiveness), "perspicacity" (perceptiveness), "munificence" (generosity), and "gregariousness" (outgoingness) all do not fit.

2. B

The key words "poor economy" tell you that you're looking for a word that means "small number." That is the definition of "dearth," so (B) is correct. "Confluence" (coming together), "glut" (excess), "spate" (large number), and "deprivation" (removal) all do not fit.

3. E

The key phrase "hundreds of songs, letters, and treatises" tells you that the word in the blank will mean something like "very productive." That is the definition of "prolific," so (E) is correct. "Condescending" (disdainful) doesn't fit with the idea of many things; neither does "lauded" (praised), "magnanimous" (generous), or "anachronistic" (in the wrong time period, ANA-, not + CHRON-, time).

4. A

The key words "reinvented" and "pioneered an entirely new style of writing" tell you that the word in the blank must mean something like

"pioneer." The word that fits most closely is "iconoclast" (radical, someone who does something groundbreaking), so (A) is correct. "Dilettante" (amateur, dabbler), "adversary," "charlatan" (faker), and "jingoist" (someone who is extremely nationalistic) all have nothing to do with the clue.

5. C

For the first blank, the fact that "simple" is paired with the blank tells you that you're looking for a word with a similar meaning. "Lofty" (high: think of a loft bed), "irate" (angry, IRA-, anger), and "adaptive" don't fit the idea of simplicity, so eliminate (A), (D), and (E). For the second blank, the key word "devoid" is a sign that this blank will be the *opposite* of simple. "Industriousness" (being hard-working) doesn't fit, but "ambiguity" (lack of clarity) does. Since "unequivocal" (clear and direct) fits well with the first blank, (C) is correct.

6. D

Start with the second blank. "Spontaneous" (impulsive) is paired with the blank, so you're looking for a positive word with a similar meaning. "Sophisticated" is positive but unrelated to spontaneity, so eliminate (A). "Egregious" (over-the-top awful) is extremely negative, so eliminate (B). "Militant" (aggressive, unwilling to compromise) is also negative, so eliminate (C) as well. For the first blank, if the writers valued spontaneous acts, they would not value revision, so you're looking for a negative word indicating dislike. "Organized" is neutral and has nothing to do with dislike, so eliminate (E). In (D), "spurned" means "rejected," and "organic" is a good synonym for "spontaneous," so (D) is correct.

7. D

Start with the first blank: the key phrase "a clear chain of command" tells you that the word in the first blank must refer to a system that contains a clear chain of command. "Incentive" (reward) clearly doesn't fit at all, and neither does "intuition" (gut feeling), so cross off (C) and (E) right away. A "democracy" is a system in which people are directly responsible for electing their officials; democratic governments do often have clear chains of command, but that is not the definition of a democracy, so you can eliminate (B). Then move on to the second blank. The key words "in fact" and "turbulent" tell you that this will contrast with the first blank, and be something opposite to well-ordered. "Summary" doesn't fit at all, so (A) is out. Even if you aren't sure what "hierarchy" (chain of command) or "amalgam" (a random jumble of stuff) means, you know (D) must be correct.

8. B

Here, the parallel structure gives you "member of no officially recognized school" for the first blank, and "odd behavior" for the second. In the first blank, you can cross off "intense" and "whimsical" (lighthearted) because they have nothing to do with the clue, so (C) and (E) are out. For the second blank, "versatile" (flexible) and "ascetic" (shunning worldly goods) don't fit, so (A) and (D) are out. That leaves (B): someone "aloof" distances himself from a group, and "eccentric" means "behaving oddly."

9. B

Start by looking at the parallel structure between the two halves of the sentence. The colon tells you that the second half will be parallel to the first. Notice how "*key* constituent of precious materials" in the second half matches well with "importance in the first." This shows you that the missing words will somehow relate to the idea that carbon makes up less than 0.1 percent of the Earth's bulk. Start with the second blank. "Density," "effectiveness," "utility" (usefulness), and "durability" (ability to last for a long time) have nothing to do with the fact that carbon makes up such a tiny percentage of the earth's bulk. Only "sparseness" (rarity) fits, and "disproportionate" works as well. The sentence is essentially saying that although carbon is very important, there isn't very much of it (i.e. it's

sparse) – so those two factors are disproportionate to one another (one is big, the other small).

10. D

The key phrase "continuing efforts are made to *prevent* its _____" tells you that the word in the second blank will mean the opposite of the first. Think also about the fact that sentence is talking about *dystopian* novels – ones that depict imaginary, often futuristic, societies in which people lead dehumanizing and fearful lives (think of *The Hunger Games*). Even if you're unfamiliar with the word "dystopian," the prefix DYS- (not) should give you a clue that it's something bad. Logically, a society in which people are unhappy would probably do bad things to families, so you can assume that the word in the first blank is negative. And since the second blank is the opposite of the first, you can assume that the correct word will be positive. Start with the first blank: "constructed," and "promoted" are positive, so eliminate (B) and (C). Now look at the second side. "Dissolution" is negative, so eliminate (E). Now you're down to (A) and (D). "Obliterated" and "eradicated" both mean "destroyed," but "resolution" isn't the opposite of destruction, so eliminate (A). That leaves (D): "eradicated" means "destroyed," which is something a dystopian society would logically do to families, and "resurgence" (revival) is the opposite. So (D) is correct.

11. E

The key word "nevertheless" tells you that the words in the two blanks will express contrasting ideas, so you're looking for a pair of opposites. In addition, since the second blank refers to Pollock's emerging artistic personality, you can assume that the word will be positive – artists usually get better as they mature. Consequently, you can assume that the word in the first blank will be somewhat negative. For the first blank, "intriguing" is positive, so eliminate (B), and for the second blank, "confounding" (confusing) is negative, so eliminate (D). "Imaginative" and "irreverent" (not serious) are both relatively positive, so eliminate (A). "Simplistic" is negative and "aesthetic" (having to do with beauty) is somewhat positive, but the two aren't opposites (the opposite of "simplistic" is "complex"), so eliminate (C). For (E), "hackneyed" (unoriginal) and "innovative" (new, groundbreaking) are opposite, so (E) is correct.

12. B

The key phrase "leftover…from the formation" and the word "original" tell you that this sentence is talking about the birth of the solar system, so you want a word that means newborn or in the process of formation. "Nascent" means "newborn," so (B) is correct. "Celestial" (relating to the heavens), "luminous" (filled with light, LUM-, light), "imperturbable" (unable to be upset), and "elliptical" (shaped like an ellipse or vague) all do not fit.

13. D

The sentence contrasts "quite energetic and productive" with the blank, so you're looking for a somewhat negative word that means the opposite of "energetic." (D) is correct because "indolence" means "laziness." "Vivacious" means "lively" (VIV-, live) so eliminate (A). "Benevolence" (kindness, goodwill, BENE-, good + VOL-, will) is positive, so eliminate (B). "Joviality" (jolliness) is also positive, so eliminate (C). And "abstemiousness" (not indulging in luxuries, particularly rich food) is not the opposite of having a lot of energy, so eliminate (E).

14. B

Looking at the sentence, it's clear that the first blank and the second blank will be similar, but the first blank will be more moderate (minor _____) and the second will be more severe (outright _____). The word "sins" lets you know they will both be negative. Looking at the first blank, "revelations" isn't negative, so (C) is out. Moving on to the second blank, "reconciliation" (bringing together) is positive,

so eliminate (A). An "indiscretion" is something unwise or not prudent, which is negative, but not a more extreme version of "platitudes" (clichés), so (D) doesn't fit either. Classification isn't negative at all, so (E) is clearly out. In choice (B), "fabrication" (outright making up lies) is a more extreme version of "inaccuracies," so (B) is correct.

15. A

The key phrase "alternately predicting" tells you that the journalist wavered, or couldn't make up his mind. To "vacillate" is to go back and forth between two possibilities, or to be indecisive, so (A) is correct. "Desisted" (backed off), theorized, "dissented" (disagreed), and "capitulated" (gave in) all do not fit.

16. E

Start with the second blank because you have more information about it. It's contrasted with "a single event," so you know the word in the second blank has to mean something like "a lot." "Paucity" (small amount) and "diminution" (decreasing amount) are both the opposite of "a lot," so eliminate (A) and (B). "Invocation" (request for help or support) has nothing to do with "a lot," so eliminate (C). Now look at the first side. The key word "struggles" tells you that you're looking for something negative. "Benign" means "harmless," which is the opposite of what you want, so eliminate (D). (E) is correct because "dire" means "serious," and "confluence" means "multiple things coming together" (CON-, with + FLU-, flow).

17. C

This sentence sets up a contrast between being overwhelmingly well-received and the second half of the sentence, so you know the second half will be negative. Start with the second blank. "Focus on the central argument" would be a good thing, but since this part of the sentence is describing something *bad* about the book, fill in a word like "take away" or "distract" in the blank. You can eliminate (A) since "extend" is positive. The scope, or range of topics covered in the book, could take away focus from the central argument only if it's too broad: the book tries to cover too many things, and so it can't focus on any one thing. So "large size" or something similar would be a good word to plug in the first blank. "Limit" is exactly the opposite of large size, so cross off (B). "Meagerness" (small amount) is also the opposite, so cross off (D) as well. Likewise, in (E), "consistency" does not mean "large size." "Breadth" does mean "large size," and "divert" means "take away," so (C) is correct.

18. B

The key phrase "diminishing their intrusion into waking life" tells you that the second blank must mean something like "reduce." Careful not to jump to (C) – "decrease" fits perfectly, but "expels" doesn't fit. Why? Because the word "paradoxically" tells you that the correct word must have something to do with exposing people to fearful memories. Logically, exposing people to fearful memories would make them *more* frightened, but *paradoxically*, the opposite would occur – people would become *less* frightened. So "expels" (gets rid of) is the opposite of what you want, and (C) doesn't work after all. The only other synonym for "reduce" is "mitigate," and "evokes" works for the first side because it is consistent with the idea of exposing people to fearful memories. Remember that in two-blank questions, you will often have more than one answer that works for one of the blanks – in those cases, it is usually the slightly harder or more obscure synonym that will be correct (e.g. "mitigate" rather than "decrease").

19. E

The city council member's behavior was unethical, so the word in the blank will be negative. This lets you cross off "lauded" (praised) and "fortified" (made stronger; think of a cereal *fortified* with Vitamin B). "Mollified" means "calmed" or "softened" (MOLL-, soft), which makes no sense. "Ousted" means

"removed," and "censured" means "criticized" or "punished," so both (D) and (E) can stay. Now look at the second side: a "delegate" is someone who performs a task on behalf of someone else, so (D) doesn't make sense. In (E), "constituents" are people who are represented by someone holding political office, so it makes sense that the city council member would be gotten rid of by the people who elected him after his misbehavior was revealed.

20. D

The information after the colon tells you that by the age of eighteen, Sackville-West had produced an enormous body of work. A "prodigious" quantity is an enormous quantity, so (D) is correct. "Renowned" (famous), "perceptive," "reclusive," and "despondent" (extremely depressed) all do not fit.

21. B

You have more information about the second blank, so start with it and work backwards. The key phrase "occur *only* when an animal is sick or provoked" tells you that you need a work that means something like "unusual." That eliminates everything except (A) and (B) because "sporadic" means "infrequent" and "anomalous" means "unusual." "Tragic" and "devastating" are words that would logically be associated with wolf attacks, but neither fits the sentence. "Mundane" means "commonplace" and does not fit at all. Now look at the first side: "present in virtually all human societies" tells you that this word must mean something like "widespread." "Imminent" means "about to occur," which does not fit. "Ubiquitous" means "everywhere," which fits with "widespread," so the answer is (B).

22. D

The sentence sets up a contrast between the two blanks, so you're looking for a pair of words that have opposite meanings. "Trite" (unoriginal) and "peripheral" (on the side, unimportant) are unrelated, so eliminate (A). "Central" and "attributed" are not opposites, so eliminate (B). "Irrelevant" and "redundant" (repetitive) are opposites, so keep (C). "Arbitrary" (irrelevant, not chosen for a particular reason) is the opposite of "essential," so keep (D). And "cryptic" (mysterious) has nothing to do with "related," so eliminate (E).

Now think about what the sentence is saying: for the first blank, if sounds rather than words dominate the poem, then the words would not seem to be very important (i.e. arbitrary), and the opposite of "irrelevant" is "relevant" or "important" – something good. "Redundant" means "repetitive," which 1) isn't the same thing as "relevant," and 2) has a negative connotation. "Essential," on the other hand, does mean "important" and has a positive connotation, so (D) is correct.

23. C

If the sentence confuses you, focus on the relationship between the words instead. The key phrase "on the contrary" tells you that the words in the two blanks will have opposing meanings. (A): "stable" is different from "retreat," so leave this answer. (B): "explicit" (absolutely clear) has no relationship to "action," so eliminate it. (C): "immutable" (can't be changed) is the opposite of "flux" (change). (D): "capricious" (unpredictable) contains a similar idea to "motion," so eliminate it. "Unintelligible" (incomprehensible) has no relationship to "demand," so eliminate (E). Now think about the two options you have left: "stable" and "immutable" have similar meanings, so you need to look at the second side to decide between them. Even if you're not really sure what the sentence is saying, you do know that it's talking about language. "Retreat" (back down) is a word that's typically used in a military context. It describes what an army does when it knows it's losing – it can't really be used to describe a language – so you can make an educated guess that (A) is not the answer. That leaves (C), which is correct.

The sentence is essentially saying that because languages change constantly (i.e. are "in flux," it is impossible to consider a single version of a language "standard" or "normal." Although words in the two blanks are opposite, they express the same *idea* – namely, that languages change. "Mutable" means "able to change," so "immutable" means "unable to change." Remember that two negatives make a positive, so "not immutable" = able to change.

24. C

The contrast between "shortcomings" (flaws) and the information in the second half of the sentence tells you that the second half will be positive. Start with the second blank. "Well-supported" is a clue that lets you cross off (A), since a "delusion" is a false idea that isn't well-supported. "Initiation" (being formally accepted into a group) doesn't fit – the sentence is talking about something that the author *believes*, and "initiation" has nothing to do with arguments or beliefs. Eliminate (D). Same problem with "volition" (desire), so eliminate (E). The fact that the first blank is linked with the second by the word "and" tells you that the first blank will be positive as well. "Apathy" (lack of interest) is negative, so eliminate (B). That leaves (C). "Exuberance" means "enthusiasm," and a "conviction" is a deeply held belief (note the second meaning), so (C) is correct.

25. E

Since the word in the first blank is an indicator of the second, the two blanks should have similar meanings. "Paragons" (perfect examples) and "inevitable" (unavoidable) aren't similar, so (A) is out. "Defects" and "plausible" (very possible) are unrelated, so (B) doesn't work either. "Expulsions" (forcing something out) doesn't make sense, so eliminate (C). "Catalysts" (substances that speed up a reaction) could fit with the idea of an earthquake, but "inert" means "not moving," so the words in (D) are opposites. "Harbingers" are warnings, and "imminent" means about to happen, so (E) is the only answer choice that fits.

26. B

If the author "shap[ed] the truth to advance his own agenda," then we know he wasn't honest. And since the word "although" sets up a contrast between the two blanks, the word in the first blank has to mean something like "honest." "Detail," "exaggeration," and "interest" all don't fit, but "candor" (directness, honesty) and "fidelity" (faithfulness, FID-, faith) both fit.

Now look at the second blank; the key word "shaping" indicates that you're looking for a word that means something like "flexible." "Malleable" fits exactly, but "reciprocal" (done in exchange for something else) does not fit at all. So the answer is (B).

27. D

The key phrase "requiring residents to move elsewhere" tells you that the word you're looking for a word that means something like "took over" or "seized." That is the definition of "expropriated" (EX-, from + PROP- as in property), so (D) is correct. "Cultivated" is a word commonly associated with land, but it doesn't fit the sentence, so eliminate (A). "Interrupted," "maintained," and "stipulated" (required) do not make sense in context, eliminating (B), (C), and (E).

28. C

The fact that Helen Thomas became a controversial figure tells you that she enjoyed asking blunt questions, so you're looking for a positive word that conveys that idea. "Disdain" (condescension), "antipathy" (dislike), "abhorrence" (loathing), and "disregard" (not caring about) are all negative. "Proclivity" (liking for) is the only word that fits, so (C) is correct.

29. A

The information after the colon tells you that Kian is a very good chess player, so you're looking for a very positive word that means something like "very good." "Adroit" means

"clever" or "highly skilled," which fits the clue. "Evasive" (hard to pin down), "execrable" (awful), and "unrepentant" (not feeling guilty about doing something bad) all do not fit, so eliminate (B)-(D). Careful with (E): "ambitious" is positive, but the sentence says nothing about what Kian hopes to achieve in chess, only that he is highly skilled at it.

30. D

This is a sentence that may seem confusing initially, so make sure you take a moment and figure out what it's really saying before you do anything. The sentence is talking about inventing alphabets for "traditionally oral languages." A language that's "traditionally oral" is one that exists only in speech and that lacks an alphabet, so if linguists are inventing alphabets, they're not just studying the language but also *changing* it. Both blanks will therefore have something to do with the idea that the inventors (i.e. the linguists) are changing the language.

Start with the first blank. You can eliminate (A) because "preserves" is the opposite of "changing." "Mimics" (copies) and "explicates" (explains) also don't have anything to do with changing, so eliminate (C) and (E) as well. Now look at the second blank: "bystander" doesn't make sense — a "bystander" is someone who watches but isn't involved, whereas if linguists are changing the language, they're involved by definition. So (B) is out. That leaves (D). Although "activist" may sound odd to you, it fits the definition of someone who is actively involved in changing a language.

31. E

The second half of the sentence lets you know that the novels fit the category of techno-thriller literature, so you could plug in "are examples of" or something similar in the blank. To epitomize something is to provide a perfect example of it, so (E) is the correct answer. "Forestall" (prevent), "sanctify" (make holy, SANCT-, holy), "mandate" (order), and "jettison" (throw away) all do not fit.

32. D

The information after the semicolon tells you that the conductor's comments must have been very harsh, so you're looking for a word that means "very harsh." Only "callousness" (cruelty) fits that definition. "Timorousness" (shyness), "banality" (lack of originality), "diffidence" (aloofness), and "inscrutability" (incomprehensibility) all do not fit.

33. E

The key phrase "subsisting with only the most basic necessities" tells you that the word in the blank must describe someone who does not need a lot of fancy things. The only word that fits that requirement is "ascetic" – someone who rejects all luxuries and lives like a monk. "Exalted" (lofty), "irascible" (easily angered), "egotistical" (narcissistic), and "oblivious" (unaware of one's surroundings) all do not fit.

34. A

The first blank since is defined at the end of the sentence – it must be a synonym for "tirade" (long and angry speech). The sentence tells you that the listeners were unprepared for something in the host's *most recent* tirade, implying that they were already accustomed to his tirades. If you know that "diatribe" is a synonym for "tirade," then you can make an educated guess that (A) is most correct. "Vitriol" means "fury," so that fits as well – the listeners were used to hearing the host rant and rave, but they were unprepared for how nasty his most recent rant was.

"Foibles" and "idiosyncrasies" both mean "quirks," which doesn't fit with the idea of a tirade, eliminating (B) and (E). In (D), "platitudes" (clichés) aren't "tirades" either. In (C), "punditry" (being a public expert on a particular topic, usually holding very strong opinions) would be a possible fit for the first blank, but "ideology" doesn't work – a pundit by definition has an ideology, so listeners wouldn't be "unprepared" for the fact that the talk-show host had one.

35. B

The sentence indicates that the word in the second blank is the result of the first, and "embarrassingly" tells you that the word in the second blank is negative. (B) is correct because it contains the only pair in which the first word would lead logically to the second. Someone who spoke "impetuously" (impulsively) would be likely to make "inapt" (inappropriate) comments. In (A), someone who spoke "judiciously" (wisely, showing good judgment) would not make "pedantic" (dull, dry, detail-obsessed) comments. (C): "phlegmatic" means "calm," which is positive, so (C) can be eliminated on that basis. (D): someone who spoke "whimsically" (frivolously, impulsively) would not make "portentous" (heavy, serious) comments – just the opposite. (E): someone who spoke "belligerently" (aggressively) would not make "sagacious" (wise) comments.

Hard (p. 44)

1. B

The sentence sets up a contrast between the way maps looked in the past and the way maps look today, so you know you're looking for a pair of opposites. (B) contains the only pair of opposites and makes sense in context. Logically, the use of computers and satellites to ensure accuracy would make maps look more similar (uniform = unvarying) which is the opposite of "eclectic" (varied). In (A), "myriad" (many) is along the same idea as "superfluous" (an excessive amount). In (C), "geographical" has nothing to do with "anachronistic." The second side also doesn't make sense. If maps were "anachronistic," they would no longer be relevant, but they *are* still relevant – they're just produced by computers, not people. In (D), "arbitrary" (not chosen for any good reason) isn't the opposite of "recondite" (obscure, understood by only a few people). And in (E), "discrete" (different, distinct) fits for the first blank, but if computers and satellites made maps *more* precise, they'd all look similar, not more "heterogeneous" (different).

2. B

Start with the second blank. The populations expand beyond the limits of their resources, so a crisis would reduce them back *within* the limits of their resources. Look for a word that means something like "smaller." "Adaptable" (flexible) and "ample" (large) don't fit, so eliminate (A) and (E). For the first blank, you need a word that could logically result in too much expansion. A population that was "vulnerable" would be wiped out quickly, so (C) is the opposite of what you want. "Inveterate" (having an ingrained habit, e.g. an *inveterate* liar) does not fit at all, so eliminate (D). In (B), "unchecked" (uncontrolled, note the second meaning) populations would logically grow beyond their resources, and "sustainable" is a good fit for reasonable, so (B) is correct.

3. C

"Gained" is a clue that the second blank will be positive and mean something like "support." "Dexterity" (flexibility) is positive but doesn't fit, so eliminate (A). "Reticence" (reluctance) is negative, so eliminate (E). Now look at the first blank. The notion has *only recently* gained support, so fill in a negative word like "doubted." "Lauded" (praised) is positive, and "exacerbated" (made worse) is negative but doesn't fit, so (B) and (D) are out. In (C), "disputed" is negative, and "traction" (acceptance – note the second meaning) works as a synonym for "support."

4. C

Start with the second blank: "rigid classical forms" would prevent creativity, so fill in a negative word like "prevent." "Enhanced" and "ameliorated" (MELIOR-, better) clearly don't fit, so eliminate (A) and (D). "Chastised" means scolded, so (B) doesn't work, either. For the first blank, "modernizing" tells you that Tagore rejected or moved beyond the classical forms, so you're looking for a word that conveys that idea. "Prevaricating" means "lying," which doesn't work. In (C), "eschewing" (rejecting) works for

the first blank, and "frustrated" works as a synonym for prevented (note the second meaning), so (C) is correct.

5. D

Start with the second blank. "Insidious" (subtly causing harm) and the fact that Ptolemy "simply made things up" tells you that you're looking for a negative word. "Illusion" is neutral and "achievement" is positive, so eliminate (B) and (C). "Anachronism" (in the wrong time) doesn't fit because the sentence says nothing about time periods. Now look at the first blank. In (A), if Ptolemy was *averse* to (disliked) an error, he wouldn't be making the error (shortcoming). (D) is correct, because someone who is "prone to" (has a tendency toward)...a "vice" (fault) would logically make up what he did not know for sure.

6. B

The sentence tells you that Whitson spent more time performing space walks than Williams, so plug in something like "beat" for the blank. "Admonished" (scolded), "scrutinized" (examined closely), "expedited" (sped up), and "obfuscated" (confused or made unclear) all do not make sense in context. "Eclipsed" means "surpassed," so (B) is correct.

7. D

The key phrase "contrasting" personalities indicates that the words in the blanks have opposite meanings. The sentence provides no information about the meaning of either word, so start by looking at the relationship between each pair of words. (A): "capricious" (unpredictable) isn't the opposite of "wistful" (longing for the past), so eliminate it. (B): "diffident" (aloof) isn't the opposite of "supercilious" (condescending), so eliminate it. (C): "reserved" (aloof) is similar to "laconic" (not talkative), so eliminate it. (D): "taciturn" (quiet) is the opposite of "gregarious" (outgoing), so keep it. (E): "credulous" (gullible) isn't the opposite of "voluble" (talkative), so eliminate it. (D) is the only possibility.

8. A

The sentence makes it clear that the coconut tree is a very useful resource ("hundreds of foods and other essential items"), so you're looking for a positive word. "Arboreal" means "related to trees" – this is technically true but doesn't fit the clue, so eliminate (B). "Trivial" means "unimportant," so eliminate (C). "Ineffable" means "inexpressible," and "auspicious" means " a good omen," neither of which makes sense in context. "Invaluable" is a tricky word because from the roots it looks like it should mean "worthless," but in reality it refers to something so precious that you can't put a price on it. Thus, (A) is correct.

9. D

The key words "help provide sustenance" tell you that the word in the first blank is positive. "Analysts" is neutral, "perpetrators" (people who commit crimes) and "skeptics" are negative, so eliminate (A), (B), and (C). "Proponents" are people who favor something, and "facilitators" make something easier. Now look at the second blank: it could help provide a lot of food if it wasn't harmed by pests, so you're looking for a word that means "can't be harmed." That is the definition of "invulnerable," so (D) is correct. "Inconsequential" means "unimportant," so (E) can be eliminated.

10. E

In this sentence, the phrase "but it was the publication of *1984* that *truly*…" tells you that the two words will be similar, and that the second will be a slightly stronger version of the first. It's not immediately clear whether the words are both positive or both negative, though, so start by looking at the relationship between each pair. (A): "misconstrued" (misunderstood) is negative, but "advocated" is positive, so eliminate it. (B): "reviled" (loathed – note that the prefix "RE-" does not mean "again" in this case) is negative, but "vindicated" is positive. (C): "lauded" is positive, but "jeopardized" (put in danger) is negative, so

eliminate it. (D): "panned" (criticized) is negative, and so is "insinuated" so keep it. (E): "extolled" (praised) is positive, as is "cemented" (solidified, finalized), so keep it.

Now plug in and think about what the sentence is saying: of the two answers remaining, you can probably start by getting rid of (D). "Insinuated" (subtly suggested bad things about) is a *weaker* version of "panned." Besides, you can *insinuate* an idea – you can't insinuate a place in history.

(E) works because having one's reputation "cemented" (the word implies permanence – think of how strong cement is) is stronger than simply being praised. So both words fit.

11. E

You have two key pieces of information in this sentence: the phrase "public displays of generosity" tells you that the word in the first blank must mean "displaying generosity," and the phrase "opponents denounced" tells you that the word in the second blank must be negative. The easiest way to narrow the answers down is to start with the first blank. An "ideologue" is someone who adheres very strictly to a particular set of beliefs, so eliminate (A). A "jingoist" is someone who's excessively nationalistic, so eliminate (B). "Idealist" (someone who puts ideals ahead of reality) is close, but it doesn't quite fit the idea of public generosity, so eliminate (C). "Mercenary" (soldier for hire) also doesn't fit, so eliminate (D). That leaves (E): an "altruist" performs charitable works for their own sake, and "machination" means "underhanded scheming."

12. D

The key words "so convincing" tell you that the word in the first blank must be positive, so start by looking at the first side. "Mendacious" (lying) and "bellicose" (aggressive) are strongly negative, so eliminate (A) and (B). "Ineluctable" (unavoidable) also doesn't fit with the idea of doing convincing impressions of people, so eliminate (E) as well. Now look at the second side. "Virtuosic" (extremely gifted) makes sense, but virtuosic impressions wouldn't automatically "assuage" (soothe people). If you tried hard enough, you could probably find a relationship between the two ideas, but the sentence doesn't explicitly indicate one. On the other hand, there is a clear cause-and-effect relationship between the two words in (D). If Sara's impressions were "preternatural" (unusual in an unnatural) way, then people would logically feel "unnerved" (freaked out) by them. So (D) is correct.

13. A

The sentence indicates that other authors portray the security officers in extreme ways (mindless vs. paranoid), so you're looking for a relatively neutral word that means something like "moderate." "Nuanced" means "making subtle distinctions," which fits as the opposite of extreme. "Perfunctory" (short, to-the-point), "consummate" (absolute), "bellicose" (aggressive, violent), and "illustrious" (well-known) all do not fit.

14. E

This sentence gives you two pieces of information: "but" tells you that the two words will have opposite meanings, and "the embodiment of life in the American Midwest" tells you that Cather's novels are strongly identified with one particular place. Start by looking at the relationship between the words. (A): "spurious" (false) isn't the opposite of "pejorative" (negative, PEJOR-, bad). (B): "provincial" (narrow-minded) isn't the opposite of "didactic" (intended to teach). (C): "exclusive" isn't the opposite of "recondite"

(esoteric, understood by few people). Careful with (D): "myopic" (narrow-minded) is negative and "compelling" is positive, but the two aren't exactly opposites. (E): "parochial" (narrow-minded) and "cosmopolitan" (open-minded) are exact opposites, and "parochial" is consistent with the idea that Cather is identified only with a particular region, so (E) is correct.

15. C

The word "once" at the beginning of the sentence establishes a contrast between the two words – in the past, the administrator believed one thing, but now she believes something else. The fact that she was originally a "proponent" (supporter) of the reforms tells you that the word in the first blank must be positive, while the word in the second blank must be negative. If you wanted to plug in your own words, you could use "enthusiastic" for the first blank, and "hates" for the second. Start with the first blank: "fervid" and "ardent" (very strong) fit, as does "unswerving" (absolutely committed), but "torpid" (lethargic) and "elusive" (hard to find or define) don't fit, so eliminate (B) and (D). Now look at the second side: you're looking for something negative. "Evokes" (recalls) is positive, as is "promulgates" (makes known), so eliminate (A) and (E). That leaves (C). "Excoriates" means "harshly criticizes," which fits with the idea of hating, so (C) is correct.

16. B

The key phrase "gave little thought to rejecting it" tells you that the actress didn't consider things very carefully when she made her decision. You can therefore plug in something like "hastily" for the blank. That is the definition of "precipitously," so (B) is correct. "Apprehensively" (nervously), "zealously" (showing strong emotion for a doctrine or cause), "parsimoniously" (stingily, cheaply), and "duplicitously" (deceptively) all do not fit.

17. D

The key phrase "entirely unmarred by any unfavorable commentary" tells you that the critics' praise was very high. "Tacit" (silent), "blithe" (carefree), "trivial" (unimportant), and "convoluted" (extremely complex) do not fit. (D) is correct because "unqualified" means absolute. In this case, the prefix UN- is not reliable.

If you're not sure about "unmarred," don't let it throw you off – the fact that sentence is talking about *unfavorable* commentary should let you make an educated guess that it means something like "not ruined" (which is in fact the definition).

18. C

Start with the first blank since you have more information about it. The key phrase "holding fiercely to his ideals" tells you that this word must mean something like "extremely stubborn." "Tenacious," "intransigent," and "obdurate" all fit this definition, but you can eliminate "exalted" (lofty) and "inscrutable" (perplexing). That leaves (A), (C), and (D). Now think about the second blank. If the first blank means "stubborn," then logically the second must refer to the fact that the subject is unwilling to acknowledge any flaws. So you're looking for a word similar to "acknowledge." "Burnish" (polish) doesn't make sense, so eliminate (A). "Expurgate" means "get rid of," which doesn't fit either, so eliminate (D). That leaves (C): "concede" means "give in," which fits with the idea of recognizing flaws. So (C) is correct.

19. B

The sentence sets up a contrast between the two blanks, so you're looking for a pair of opposites. Since there is no information about the definition of either word, start by looking at the relationship between each pair of words. (A): "ignored" is not the opposite of "inconsequential" (unimportant, lit. having no consequences), so eliminate it. (B): "savaged"

(attacked) is the opposite of "unscathed" (unharmed), so keep it. (C): "assuaged" (soothed) is not the opposite of "definitive" (absolute), so eliminate it. (D): "scoffed at" (disdained) is not the opposite of "cryptic" (perplexing, unforthcoming), so eliminate it. (E): "censured" (punished) is not the opposite of "unexceptional" (normal, usual). That leaves (B) as the only possibility.

20. C

For the first blank, "accused" tells you the word will be negative, and "directly from the author's own life rather than her imagination" gives you a hint about what the negative word will be: you want something that means "unimaginative." "Auspicious" (good omen), "ephemeral" (short-lived), and "timorous" (shy, afraid) all do not make sense. Be careful with (E): "individualistic" means "acting without worrying about what other people think" – it has nothing do with not being original. "Abscond" (sneak away) also doesn't fit. In (C), "derivative" does mean "unoriginal," and "stem" means "develop from" (note the second meaning).

21. C

The experiment was failing, so the researchers decided to do something until they could find a better way to run the experiment (a more effective methodology). For the first blank, try plugging in something like "produce." (B), (C), and (D) all work, but "stipulate" (require), and "withhold" don't make sense, so eliminate (A) and (E). For the second blank, a word like "stop" or "put on hold" would make sense to fill in. "Assuage" (calm, soothe) clearly doesn't fit. "Ostracize" (exclude from a group) is negative, but it doesn't have quite the right meaning; it can also only be used to refer to a person. "Table" means "postpone," so (C) is correct.

22. E

The key words "notorious" and "dismissed" tell you that both words will be negative. In addition, "overblown rhetoric" tells you that the word in the first blank will mean something like "overblown." "Sensationalistic," "pretentious," and "bombastic" all fit, but "caustic" (harsh, burning) and "ponderous" (serious, weighty) don't, so eliminate (A) and (D). Now look at the second side. The fact that the senator's colleagues "dismissed" this word means that they probably didn't take him too seriously. "Diffidence" (aloofness) and "subjectivity" don't make sense, so eliminate (B) and (C). (E) is correct because "bluster" means "empty and overblown words," which fits with the idea of the senator's speeches not being taken seriously.

23. B

The sentence sets up a contrast between the two blanks, so you know you're looking for a pair of opposites. In addition, the key phrase "also has curative properties" tells you that the word in the first blank must be negative and mean the opposite of "curative" (i.e. harmful). "Soporific" (inducing sleep), "mollifying" (calming), "unanticipated" (unexpected), and "palliative" (lessening pain) all do not fit. That leaves only (B): "adverse" means "harmful," and "exploit" means "take full advantage of." Note that this word often has a negative connotation but can be used positively in this sense.

24. B

The sentence indicates that Lucinda does not _____ to anyone's point of view even when she is mistaken, so plug in something like "stubborn" for the first blank. "Capricious" (unpredictable), "equivocal" (unclear), "quiescent" (quiet), and "tractable" (agreeable) all do not fit, leaving (B) as the only option.

25. E

The sentence sets up a contrast between the words in the two blanks, so you know you're

looking for a pair of opposites. The key word "callow" (youthful, naïve) tells you that the first blank must have a similar meaning, while "profound" tells you that the second blank will be positive and mean the opposite. Start with the first blank. "Superficial," "naïve," and "ingenuous" (naïve) all fit, but "meticulous" (detailed-oriented) and "terse" (succinct) don't work, so eliminate (A) and (D). Now look at the second blank. "Buoyant" means "uplifting," which isn't the opposite of "superficial," and neither is "atonement" (repentance), so eliminate (B) and (C). That leaves (E): "erudition" (deep knowledge) fits as the opposite of "callow," so (E) is correct.

Set 1 (p. 48)

1. B

The key phrase is "well over 100 years old," which indicates that the word in the blank must have something to do with old age. "Longevity" is the only word that fits: look at "long" to give you a clue what this word might mean. "Amplitude" (large size), "graciousness" (politeness), "severity" (harshness), and "sluggishness" (slowness) do not fit.

2. D

The sentence essentially requires you to define the word "pragmatic" – if you know that it means "practical," then you can jump right to (D). Otherwise, the phrase "should not be viewed as abstract truths but rather..." indicates that the word in the blank must mean the opposite of "abstract," again leading you to (D). "Immediate," "severe," "felicitous" (lucky) and "unintentional" are all words *related* to consequences, but none of them is the direct opposite of "abstract" the way "practical" is.

3. E

Tiwanaku changed from something "locally dominant" into a _____ state," so the blank must be the opposite of "locally dominant." The second half of the sentence gives you another clue: "conquered its neighbors" indicates the word in the blank will have something to do with seizing power. A monarchical and a democratic don't fit because these are just different forms of government, which the sentence doesn't talk about at all, so cross off (B) and (D). For the second blank, try filling in a word like spread: this lets you cross off subsumed (note the prefix SUB-, under), and evaluated. In choice (E), imperialist fits with powerful, and disseminated (look at the root words DIS-, out from, + SEM-, seed) means spread, so you're left with (E) as the correct answer.

4. B

The clue is "largely self-taught," so you want a word that defines that means "self-taught." That is the definition of "autodidact" (AUTO-, self + didact, teach). A pedant is someone who is very knowledgeable about a subject but talks about it in a very dry and boring way, which doesn't fit the clues. An extrovert is someone very sociable and outgoing, so (C) doesn't fit. A pacifist (look at the root word PAC, peace) is someone who doesn't believe in war, and a charlatan is a fraud, so (D) and (E) don't fit either.

5. C

For the first blank, the clue is "detached:" you want a word that means something like "detachment." "Hackneyed" (unoriginal) doesn't make sense, and "convoluted" (complicated) doesn't work either, so cross off (B) and (D). "Diffident," "aloof," and "analytical" are all general synonyms for "detached." Now look at the second blank. The sentence contrasts the two blanks, so you're looking for the opposite of "detached" – something like "emotional." "Reticent" (reserved) is close in meaning to "detached," so eliminate (A). "Poignant" means "touching" or "moving," which works, so keep (C). "Vapid" (empty) doesn't work, so eliminate (E). That leaves (C).

Set 2 (p. 48)

1. D

The sentence contrasts "_____ stone tools" with "more sophisticated technologies," so the first blank must mean something like "unsophisticated," and the second must be related to "sophisticated." Start with the first blank: "fragile," "simple," and "primitive" are all related to being "unsophisticated," but (C) and (E) don't make sense. Now look at the second side. You want something that *does* fit with sophisticated technologies. "Enigmatic" (mysterious) and "elusive" ("difficult to find or understand") don't work. "Complex" works for "sophisticated," and primitive works as the opposite. So (D) works.

2. A

Start with the second blank. The compositions are original because "they successfully _____ many separate musical traditions," so try "blend" or "mix" as your own word. This lets you cross off delineate (which means outline; look at the word LINE in the middle of the word), and undermine (attack in an underhanded way) so eliminate (C) and (D). For the first blank, you also want a word that means something like "blend" or "mix," so you can cross off diffusion (which means spreading; think of the same root DIFF- in words like different) and cacophony (look at the root word PHON-, sound). "Synthesis" and "integrate" indicate mixing (look at the root SYN-, together), so (A) is correct.

3. D

For the first blank, the key phrase "only for topics of unusual importance" indicates that the first blank must mean something like "rarely." The word "however" indicates that the word in the second blank will mean the opposite of that in the first blank, so try plugging in "common." Starting with the second blank, you can eliminate (A) and (E) because "deliberate" and "innovative" do not mean "rare." Now look at the first blank: "impulsively" (suddenly, without warning) has nothing to do with "rarely," likewise for "belatedly," so you can eliminate (B) and (C). That leaves (D), which fits perfectly. "Sporadically" means "irregularly" or "infrequently," and "frequent" is its opposite.

4. B

The key phrase "one so stunning it could not be fully captured in words" tells you that the word in the blank will be strongly positive and mean something like "inexpressible" or "beyond words." That is the definition of "ineffable," so (B) is correct. "Churlish" mean "rude," which doesn't work. "Monumental" might be tempting because it looks similar to "mountain," but this word doesn't denote something inexpressible, so (C) isn't a good fit. For "prescient" (having knowledge of events before they occur), the prefix PRE-, before, suggests that this word doesn't have the correct meaning. "Ominous" means "threatening," so (E) doesn't work, leaving (B).

5. D

The construction "not only… but downright" tells you that the second blank will be a more extreme version of the first. "Inane" means "pointless" or "foolish," which is the opposite of "erudite" (extremely knowledgeable) so (A) doesn't work. "Lucid" (clear; note the root word LUC-, light) and "nebulous" (vague) are also not synonyms. "Quixotic" (ridiculously idealistic) and "fortuitous" (lucky) don't fit as synonyms either. Myopic means short-sighted, and pedantic means showing off one's knowledge, so these words are closer than the others but still not synonyms, and you can eliminate (E). In choice (D), "polemical" (divisive, think of people being at opposite poles) is a more extreme version of "contentious" (causing arguments), so (D) is correct.

Set 3 (p. 49)

1. B

The key phrase is "composing in the moment," indicating that the word in the blank must have that definition. That is the definition of "improvisation," so (B) is correct. Since the sentence is about music, (A) is tempting if you know the root word PHON-, sound, but CACO- is another root word that means bad, and an unpleasant sound has nothing to do with composing in the moment. For (C), think of the word "exhibit" hidden inside "exhibitionism:" putting something on display also doesn't work with your clue. "Recapitulation" might be an unfamiliar word, but shorten it to the abbreviation "recap," and it might look more familiar: a brief summary has nothing to do with composing in the moment. Collaboration (working together; think of the prefix COLL-, meaning with, plus the root word LABOR, "work") also doesn't fit, so cross off (E). That leaves only (B).

2. B

The key words "breathing new life" tell you that this must have been a very good speech. Try filling in "energized" for the blank. That is the definition of "galvanized," so (B) is correct. "Dissuaded" (discouraged) and "obligated" (required) clearly don't fit. Be careful with (D) and (E). "Perpetuated" means "continued," but it's the campaign that got continued, not the *supporters*. In (E), "enfranchised" means gave the vote, so even though it's related to the political context, it doesn't fit the clues.

3. B

From the sentence, you can tell that the two blanks will be similar in meaning, since the first is the result of the second. The key phrase "unexpected juxtaposition of forms" gives you a good idea of the type of word you're looking for. You could even plug in "uniqueness" and "varied," to keep the question simple. Start with the first blank. If you know that "innocuous" means "harmless" (note the negative prefix IN- and the root word NOC-, harm), you can cross off (A). "Uncanny" (mysterious or inexplicably strange) doesn't fit, so (C) can be eliminated. "Distinctive," "unusual" and "striking" fit, so keep (B), (D), and (E). Now look at the second blank. "Pedestrian" (boring) and "utilitarian" (designed to be useful rather than beautiful) both don't fit, so that leaves (B). "Distinctive" matches "unique," and "eclectic" means varied.

4. C

The key phrase "no physical evidence of them survives today" tells you that word in the blank must mean something like "temporary." "Decorous" (polite) doesn't fit. "Picturesque" means "pretty as a picture," which has nothing to do with the clue, so cross out (B). "Monstrous" is clearly a poor fit. While the masks may have been sacred, that's not what the clue indicates, so cross off (E). "Ephemeral" means "short-lived," so (C) is correct.

5. D

For the first blank, "rarely touched on serious events" tells you that what Plutarch *did* recount were unimportant things. "Serene" (calm), "apocryphal" (of doubtful authenticity), and "austere" (stern, severe, undecorated) don't fit, so eliminate (B), (C), and (E). For the second blank, the _____ accomplishments are the same as the serious events, so you want a word that means important or something similar. Be careful with (A): Roman culture is considered "classical," but the word means "traditional," not "serious." In (D), "trivial" means "unimportant," and "venerable" means "worthy of great respect," which fits the clue.

Set 4 (p. 49)

1. C

The key phrases "the world's foremost orchestras" and "numerous international awards" make it clear that Uchida is very famous, so plug in something like "famous" or "celebrated" for the blank. "Acclaimed" means "celebrated," so (C) is correct. Be careful with (A) and (E): Uchida is clearly musical, and it's reasonable to assume that she's versatile (flexible) as well, but the word you want must have something to do with *fame*, and neither "musical" nor "versatile" fits that requirement. In (B), "flamboyant" means "colorful and slightly outrageous," which doesn't fit at all. "Unnerving" means "disturbing," so (D) is out, but even if you don't know what it means, the root UN- indicates that it's something negative.

2. B

The key phrases "contrary to popular belief" and "but rather" tell you that the two blanks will be opposites, and "at length" tells you that the second word will mean something that is done slowly. For the first blank, try filling in "quickly" for your own word, since it's the opposite of "at length." "Cautiously," "intentionally," "diplomatically," and "prudently" (practically) don't have to do with speed or doing something too fast, which lets you cross off every answer choice except (B). In choice (B), "impulsively" means "react without thinking." "Deliberated" means "thought about carefully," the opposite of "impulsively," so (B) is correct.

3. D

The key phrase "almost never view humans as prey" indicates that the word in the blank must mean something like "aggressive" or "violent." That is the definition of "bellicose" (BELL, war), so (D) is correct. "Magnanimous" (generous), "conniving" (scheming), "timid" (shy) and "capricious" (unpredictable) all have nothing to do with aggression.

4. A

The sentence contrasts "*outwardly* appear[ing] to have little in common" with the word in the blank, so you're looking for something that means "hidden." That is essentially the definition of "latent" (not outwardly apparent), so (A) is correct. "Essential" (necessary), "trivial" (unimportant), "misleading," and "tacit" (silent) do not fit with the idea of something hidden.

5. E

The second blank is the cause of the first blank, so both blanks will have similar meanings: either the law will *prevent* new buildings and thus *stop* the city's growth (negative), or it will *encourage* new buildings and thus *help* the city's growth (positive). So start by looking at the relationship between the words. "Mitigated" means made less bad, which doesn't fit with "encouraging." "Restricted" is negative, but "converging" (coming together) is positive; however "converging the construction of new buildings" doesn't make sense. "Facilitated" (made easy; look at the root FACIL-, easy) and "curtailing" (preventing) are opposites. "Exculpated" means "found not guilty," which doesn't fit, so (D) doesn't work. For "circumscribed," look at the root words CIRCUM-, around, and SCRIB-, write: this means given strict boundaries, which fits with "restricting." Thus, (E) is correct.

Set 5 (p. 50)

1. C

The sentence contrasts the initial state of disrepair with the current state of being partially _____, so you know the blank will mean something like "repaired" or "put back together." "Inspired" doesn't fit; neither does "commanded," so cross off (A) and (B). "Targeted" has nothing to do with repairing, and neither does "revealed," so eliminate (D) and (E) as well. "Restored" fits perfectly with the idea of repair as well as the key words "original appearance" in the second half of the sentence.

2. E

"Public health workers" is a clue for this sentence. Public health workers want to _____ the _____ of diseases, so try filling in "stop the spread" or similar words for the blanks. For the first blank, "stimulate" and "identify" don't work, so cross off (B) and (D). Careful with (C): it's logical that public health workers would want to diagnose diseases, but the sentence provides no information about how throwing Dixie Cups away after a single use would allow them to do so. For the second blank, a prognosis is a prediction of the future course of a disease, so (A) doesn't work. In (E), "mitigate" means "reduce," and "transmission" means "spread," so (E) is correct.

3. A

The sentence sets up an opposition between the "most important spaces" and the first blank, which must logically mean something like "unimportant." If you are able to recognize (or identify by process of elimination) that "ancillary" (secondary, less important) is the only word that fits that definition, you can jump to (A). "Relegated" means "put in an inferior position," which fits perfectly. Otherwise, "luminous" (filled with light, LUMEN-, light), "contemporary," "flexible" and "cavernous" do not mean "unimportant," and thus (B)-(E) can be eliminated.

4. C

The key phrase "immediately elicit intense emotions" tells you that the blank will mean something like "intense" or "emotional." "Phlegmatic" (calm) is the opposite of what you want. "Dubious" (doubtful; look at the root word DUB-, doubt), doesn't fit either. "Implacable" (refusing to calm down, IM-, not, + PLAC-, peace) and "explicit" don't fit the clue either. "Visceral" refers to a gut feeling, so (C) is correct.

5. B

For the first blank, the key words "accused of" let you know that you need a negative word. Diplomacy is positive, so you can cross off (C). The words "on the contrary" let you know that the second blank will be a contrasting idea, so this blank will be positive. Elusive means "hard to catch or understand," which is negative. "Surreptitious" means "secretive," which isn't usually a good thing when used to describe politicians, and "terse" means concise, so (A), (D), and (E) are out. In choice (B), "obfuscate" means "make less clear," and "frank" means "honest and direct," so these two words fit.

Set 6 (p. 51)

1. D

The sentence contrasts the old (500 BC) with the new (twentieth century), so you want a word in the blank that means old. "Obscure" (unknown) might be tempting, but the sentence implies that we *do* actually know the yo-yo's roots, so (A) doesn't fit. "Diverse," "unexpected," and "fascinating" may all be true, but they don't fit the clue. Ancient means extremely old, so (D) is correct.

2. C

A model developed "entirely without experiment" doesn't sound very promising, but the sentence indicates that it was "eventually _____," so you know the first word will be positive and mean something like "accepted." This lets you cross off (A) and, if you know what "jettisoned" (rejected) means, (E). The second blank gives the reason why the theory was accepted, so this will be positive as well. "Trivial" means "unimportant," so (B) is out. If you weren't sure about "jettisoned," you can get rid of (E) now because "arrogant" is negative. In (D), "imaginative" is positive, but scientific theories do not get accepted because they're imaginative. In (C), "embraced" is positive, and "convincing" is a good reason people might have that positive reaction, so (C) is correct.

3. D

The clue for the second blank is "only a handful of speakers," so the blank should mean something like "endangered." By contrast, the first blank should mean something like "not endangered." For the first blank, "fragile" is the opposite of the word you're looking for, so eliminate (A). "Banal" (unoriginal) and "ambiguous" (unclear) also don't fit, so eliminate (B) and (E). Now look at the other side. For the second blank, "aberrant" (unusual in a bad way doesn't fit), so eliminate (C). (D) is correct: "robust" means "healthy," which contrasts with "tenuous" (just barely holding on).

4. C

"A radical break with architectural tradition" is the key phrase, giving you a hint about the connotation of the word. "Untraditional" might be a good word to fill in the blank. A reactionary is an extreme conservative, which is the opposite of the clue. An aesthete is just someone concerned with design in general; this doesn't have the connotation of breaking with tradition, so (B) doesn't work. An indigent is someone very poor, and a cosmopolitan is a world citizen or someone free of local prejudice, so (D) and (E) also don't fit. A maverick is someone who breaks with tradition, so (C) is correct.

5. A

For the first blank, the phrase "stubbornness, even _____" tells you that the word in the first blank will mean a more extreme form of stubbornness. "Intractability" (IN- + TRACT, drag) and "intransigence" both mean "extremely stubborn," so keep (A) and (E) and cross out (B)-(D). "Obtuseness" (dullness/stupidity), "alacrity" (intelligence), and "resilience" (ability to bounce back from failure) all don't fit. Now look at the second side. "Vapidity" (emptiness, stupidity) clearly doesn't fit, so eliminate (E). That leaves (A), which works since "eloquence" means "articulateness."

Set 7 (p. 51)

1. C

The key phrase "equally accessible to all its citizens" indicates that the blank will have something to do with equality. "Egalitarian" means "intended to promote equality," so (C) is correct. "Colossal" (enormous), "distant," "urban" (related to cities), and "pastoral" (related to the country) all do not fit that definition.

2. D

If the children will only try new foods after they get used to them, you know that the word in the blank will be negative and mean something like "afraid" or "suspicious of." "Wary" means suspicious of or unsure about, so (D) is correct. All of the other options are positive and can be eliminated on that basis, so if you don't know what "wary" means, you can still make a very educated guess based on process of elimination.

3. B

For the first blank, "cooler layers sinking and warmer ones rising above them" gives you a clue that the word will mean something like "arranged" in layers. "Hypnotic" doesn't have anything to do with layers, so eliminate (A). "Convoluted" (look at the root words CON-, with, and VOLUT-, turn) means "extremely complicated," which doesn't fit either. "Vacuous" (as in a vacuum) means "empty" or "banal," so eliminate (D). "Transitory" (short-lived, think of a transition) doesn't work either. For the second blank, if ceiling fans heat rooms, they should move or push the warm air from the ceiling to the floor, so "move" would be a good word to fill in the blank. In choice (B), stratified does mean arranged in layers, and circulating means moving (look at the root word CIRC-, around, as in circle), so (B) is correct.

4. C

The phrase "*so* complete *that*" tell you that the second word must be the result of the first. Because you don't have a lot of information about what the words themselves mean, you need to look carefully at the relationship between the pair of words in each answer choice and determine whether the first one would cause the second.

Start with (A): if the company "dominated" (had complete control over) the market, its brand name couldn't be "abhorred" (hated) by the product itself – products can't hate anything. (B): An "appraisal" (evaluation) wouldn't automatically cause the brand name to be "confused" with the product – there's no relationship. (C): if the company had a monopoly (total control) of the market, then yes, that would cause its brand name to become "synonymous with" (the same as) the actual product. Think of a brand like Kleenex– facial tissues are typically referred to as Kleenex, whether or not they're actually made by that company. But if you're not sure about (C), move onto (D): a company can't really "embody" a market, so the first blank doesn't really work, at any rate, that wouldn't cause its brand name to be "surpassed" by the product. That doesn't make any sense. (E): "Abandonment" and "captivated" are opposites, so one cannot cause the other. That leaves (C) as the only option.

5. B

The key word is *origin*, so fill in a word like "created" for the blank. "Collated" (gathered together) doesn't work here; neither does "desiccated" (dried up), "oriented" (turned in a specific direction), or "propelled." In (B), forged does mean created, so (B) is correct. Note the second meaning here: "forge" is more commonly used to mean "fake."

Set 8 (p. 52)

1. E

Try filling in used up or something similar in the blank. "Emaciated" means excessively thin, which doesn't make sense. Abducted (look at the roots AB-, away + DUCT-, carry) means kidnapped, and nobody can kidnap their own supplies. "Replenished" means "refilled," which is the opposite of what you want, and the hikers weren't sending their supplies to any foreign countries, so "exported" doesn't work either. "Depleted" means "used up," so (E) is correct.

2. B

The words "one legal system" gives you a clue about the first blank. Heterogeneous (look at the roots HETERO-, other and GEN-, tribe or race) means having many different parts, which is exactly the opposite of what you want, so eliminate (A). The Spanish Empire may or may not have been a constitutional monarchy, but this is never mentioned in the sentence, so eliminate (C). Likewise, "conservative" and "absolutist" may be true, but they don't fit the blank, so eliminate (D) and (E). In choice (B), united fits with one legal system. The second blank contrasts with the first, so discrete (different) fits perfectly, and (B) is correct.

3. A

The sentence indicates that animals that live on islands cannot escape when environmental disasters occur, so logically the blank must contain a negative word meaning something like "likely to be harmed by." That is the definition of "vulnerable," so (A) is correct. "Indifferent" and "insensitive" (not caring about) are negative but do not work because logically, animals would be strongly affected by environmental disasters from which they could not escape. Eliminate (B) and (D). "Inured" means "unaffected by," which is the opposite of what you want, eliminating (C). And "crucial" (very important) is positive, eliminating (E).

4. A

The key words "moral lessons" tell you that the word in the blank will have something to do with teaching morality. "Inflexible" doesn't work. "Conciliatory" means "making peace" and "recondite" means "abstruse" or "requiring highly specialized knowledge to understand," so these words don't match either. "Flippant" means "shallow" or "lacking seriousness," which also doesn't work in the blank. "Didactic" means "intended to teach," so (A) is correct.

5. D

You don't have much to go on for the first blank, so start with the second blank. The key phrase "made her the subject of much gossip" tells you that Isabella Stewart Gardner went against social convention, so you're looking for a word that captures that idea. "Embrace" and "grasp" clearly don't fit, and "condone" (overlook bad behavior) doesn't work either. This lets you cross off (B), (C), and (E). For the first blank, "eccentricity" is strangeness, which is something that would be associated with Isabella, so you're looking for a word that's generally positive. "Disdain" means dislike, which is strongly negative, so (A) doesn't work. "Penchant" means "inclination toward" or "liking for," which fits with the first blank, and "flout" means "openly reject" or "scoff at," which fits for the second blank.

Set 9 (p. 53)

1. D

The word "but" indicates that the two parts of the sentence will express opposing ideas. The word in the first blank must convey an idea that contrasts with "congregating in groups." What's the opposite of being in a group? Being alone, i.e. "solitary" (think about the root SOL-, which means "alone"). So (D) is the only possible answer. "Intimidating" (frightening), "noble," "devious" (crafty), and "curious" *could* be used to describe grizzly bears but are inconsistent with the meaning indicated by the sentence.

2. C

The key words "genetically identical" clue you in that the distinction will be "small" or "not important." "Adaptive" has nothing to do with unimportance, so eliminate (A). "Biological" doesn't make sense because the distinction *isn't* biological (they're genetically the same), so eliminate (B). In (D), profound (deep) is exactly the opposite of small, and "arcane" (obscure, understood by very few people) has nothing to do with unimportance. "Arbitrary" means "not based on any good reason," which works for the blank, so (C) is correct.

3. C

The key phrase "recycle themes and plotlines from his earlier works" lets you know the blank will mean something like "repetitive." "Pessimistic" means expecting the worst, which doesn't fit. "Intriguing" means "fascinating," so (B) doesn't work. "Prurient" means "titillating," so (D) has nothing to do with the clue, and "succinct" means short or concise, so (E) doesn't fit either. "Derivative" means "copied" or "unoriginal," which fits with the clue.

4. C

The sentence contrasts "delicate flavor" with "_____ creatures," and "high tolerance for the toxins" is an additional clue telling you that the blank will mean something like "tough." That is the definition of "hardy," so (C) is correct. "Benign" (harmless), "auspicious" (good omen), and "voracious" (having a huge appetite) all do not fit the clue. Be careful with (E): even though shrimp live in the water, "aquatic" has nothing to do with being tough.

5. D

The key words "experienced at controlling their emotions" suggest that the lie detectors are not accurate. Since the first blank describes what the lie detectors have *failed* to gain, you're looking for a positive word – you could plug in "support" or something similar. "Suspicion" is

the opposite of what you want, and "interest" doesn't quite fit with the idea of support, so (B) and (C) are out. For the second blank, you know you want a reason why the lie detectors would be bad, and people experienced at controlling their emotions gives you a hint that the word will mean something like "tricked." "Exonerated" means cleared of blame, which doesn't make sense, and "imitated" doesn't work either. "Currency" means "popularity" or "acceptance" (note the second meaning), and "duped" means tricked, so (D) is correct.

Set 10 (p. 53)

1. E

The key phrase "stamping out the disease" indicates that the word in the blank must have a similar but stronger meaning. Try plugging in something like "gotten rid of" or "eliminated." "Eradicated" (destroyed) fits that definition, so (E) is correct. "Understood," "excluded" (shut out), and "detected" clearly do not mean "destroyed," so eliminate (A)-(C). Careful with (D): if the disease were contained, it would still exist – it would simply be stopped from spreading. The sentence, however, tells you that the disease has been largely "stamped out," implying that it will no longer exist at all in the near future.

2. C

The key phrase "to fit their environments" tells you that the societies are changing their lifestyles, so you're looking for a word that means "changing." "Creating" and "verifying" (confirming the truth of: look at the root word VER-, truth) don't fit, so eliminate (B) and (E). For the second blank, the sentence is describing a shift from an initial change to something that becomes part of a culture, so a word like "established" would be a good fit. For peripheral, look at PERI-, around: this word means around the outside or not important, so it's not what you want. Eliminate (A). "Ingenious" means clever – the behaviors *could* be clever, but that's not the definition the sentence indicates, so (D) is also out. In choice (C), "adapting" means "changing," and "ingrained" means "firmly fixed," so (C) is correct.

3. C

For the first blank, the Milky Way's name is clearly appropriate because it's a "solid, milky white band," so try filling in "fits with" as your own word. "Precludes" (prevents), "belies" (contradicts), "scrutinizes" (examines closely) and "determines" all don't fit, so eliminate (A), (B), (D) and (E). (C) fits exactly with the sentence: if stars can't be distinguished because the Milky Way is a solid band, then logically its name *reflects* that fact.

4. A

The sentence contrasts "only a few have *proven* _____" (good) to the "power of *self-delusion*" (bad), so you know the word in the first blank is positive. "Components" just means "parts," so (C) is out. "Caveats" (warnings) also clearly doesn't fit, so eliminate (E) as well. For the second blank, the sentence tells you that most supplements are popular *because* of self-delusion, so there's going to be a positive relationship between those words. "Comparison" is neutral, so eliminate (B), and "refutation" is negative, so eliminate (D). That leave (A): "benefits" works with the idea of having good effects, and a "testament to" (evidence or proof of) the power of self-delusion makes sense in context.

If you're still not sure you understand, think of it this way: the sentence is basically saying that only a few dietary supplements are helpful, and the fact that people buy useless ones anyway is evidence that they can delude (fool) themselves into believing things are good for them, even when there's no evidence to indicate that that's the case.

5. B

The sentence contrasts science fiction novels with scientific consensus, describing how real scientists dismiss mental telepathy. Using the contrast between fact and fiction, try filling in "nonsense" or a similar word for the blank. "Chicanery" means "fraudulence," which is the answer closest in meaning. "Alacrity" (liveliness, willingness), "publicity," "tenacity" (stubbornness), and "monotony" (repetitiveness, dullness, MONO-, one + TONOS-, sound) all do not fit.

Set 11 (p. 54)

1. D

They key phrase is "built by no other Native American tribe," so you're looking for a word related to that idea. If you can plug in "unique," you're done. If not, "identical," "vulnerable" (open to attack), and "dependent" don't fit. The Navajo might appreciate the hogans, but that's not what the clue is asking for, so resist the temptation to pick (E). In choice (D), "unique" best fits the clue.

2. C

From the sentence, it's clear that Roosevelt and the arborists were both working towards the same goal (they were both planting trees), but while Roosevelt was creating large forests, the arborists were working on a smaller scale. This gives you a clue that the second blank should mean something along the lines of "small-scale" or "local." "Invasive" and "exclusive" are clearly wrong, so cross out (A) and (E). For the first blank, you want a word that has something to do with supporting each other, so you're looking for something positive. That eliminates (D) because "obliterated" (destroyed completely) is negative. "Defined" is neutral and also doesn't have anything to do with supporting, so you can eliminate (B) as well. (C) is correct because "supplement" means "add onto" and "modest" means "limited" or "moderate" (note the use of the second meaning here).

3. D

The key word "although" sets up a contrast between the actual language and the handwriting. The handwriting is difficult, so you know you need a positive word for the first blank. "Ineffable" means inexpressible (something you can't put into words), and "convoluted" means "excessively complex," so (B) and (E) don't work. Now look at the second side. Logically, it should mean something like "understand." "Extol" means "praise," and "initiate" means "start," neither of which fits, so eliminate (A) and (C). That leaves (D), which fits because "decipher" (make sense out of) is consistent with the idea of understanding.

4. C

The sentence contrasts the "_____ London streets" with "the far more _____ mountains," so you know the words will be opposites. "Bustling" (busy) and "fastidious" (excessively particular about details) aren't opposites, so eliminate (A). "Placid" (look at the root word PLAC-, peace) and "idyllic" are synonyms, so (B) is out. "Tranquil" and "serene" both mean "calm," so you can cross off (D). "Chaotic" and "irreverent" (not serious, IR-, not + Reverent, deeply respectful) aren't opposites either, so (E) doesn't fit. "Gritty" (grimy and urban) is a good opposite for bucolic (rural), and the words fit in the blanks (gritty London streets makes sense, as does bucolic mountains), so (C) is correct.

5. B

Start with the first blank. The sentence sets up a contrast between the work that was "once widely praised and is now being _____," so you know the first blank will be negative. "Extolled" means "praised," which is the opposite of what you're looking for, so cross off (C). "Probed" means examined, which isn't negative, so cross off (D). Now look at the second blank, although you do have some information: if you know that the scientist's work is now seen as bad, and "shoddiness"

(poorly done) is bad, then the word in the blank must indicate some sort of association with shoddiness – it might not be positive, but it won't be negative. "Antithesis" means "opposite," so you can eliminate (A). "Epitome" means "essence," which fits, so keep (B). "Forerunner" just doesn't make any sense – the sentence says nothing about one thing coming before another. So the answer is (B).

Set 12 (p. 54)

1. E

"All art forms would…be brought together" is your clue for the blank: try plugging in "complete" or something similar for the blank. "Comprehensive" means "including everything" (look at the prefix COM-, with), so (E) is correct. "Durable" (long-lasting), "peculiar" (odd), "renowned" (famous), and "stunning" (extremely beautiful) all do not fit.

2. A

The key words "by force" and "seized" tell you that Darius took the throne violently. Thus, he would have gotten rid of the heir in some negative way, so try filling in "got rid of" or a similar word for the blank. "Defended" doesn't work, and "appeased" (calmed) is also a poor fit for the clues, so cross off (B) and (E). For the second blank, if he violently took down the heir and seized the throne by force, his rise to power would be wrong, so try filling in "illegal" or a similar word. That is the definition of "illicit," and "deposed means took down by force (DE-, down, + POS, as in position), so (A) is correct. "Cursory" means quick, or not thorough, which doesn't fit, and "benevolent" (look at the roots BENE-, good, + VOL-, desire) clearly doesn't work, so (C) and (D) can be eliminated.

3. C

In this sentence, the key word "rank" tells you that the word in the first blank mean something like "rank" or "status." "Restrictions" and "relations" don't fit with this clue, so eliminate

(B) and (E). In (D), non-human societies probably wouldn't have institutions, so you can assume that's wrong as well. For the second blank, the sentence contrasts "do exist" with the "less _____" role in chimpanzee society, so try filling in a word like "important" for the blank. "Elusive" (hard to catch) doesn't make sense, so (A) is out. In choice (C), "hierarchies" means "systems of rank," and "prominent" means "important," so (C) is correct.

4. E

If "multiple perspectives do not _____ into a single view," the blank should mean something like "combine." Start with the first blank. Careful not to pick (A) without looking at the second side; "coalesce" fits perfectly, but "rigidity" is the opposite of flux (change). In (B), "palliate" (reduce pain) has nothing whatsoever to do with the clue. "Merge" also has the right meaning, but "profundity" (profoundness) isn't the opposite of coming together into a single view so (C) isn't right either. In (D), "evade" is the opposite of coming together, so that can be eliminated. In (E), "cohere" (become coherent) fits, and "ambiguity" is its opposite, so (E) is correct.

5. C

The sentence contrasts "outrageous plotlines and wooden acting" (negative) with the two blanks, so you know you're looking for two positive words. You can also tell from the word "even" that the second blank will be a slightly stronger version of the first. Using just the second blank, you can eliminate (B), (D) and (E) because "prosaic" (boring), "sanctimonious" (hypocritically self-righteous), and "caustic" (mean-spirited) are all negative. In (A), both words are positive, but "decorous" (polite) isn't a stronger version of "insightful." In (C), "sharp" can mean clever, and "trenchant" is a stronger form of the same idea, so (C) is correct.

Set 13 (p. 55)

1. A

The word "supporters" gives you a hint for the first blank: supporters don't want a law to be "overturned" or "abolished," so (C) and (E) don't fit. For the second blank, try filling in your own word. Remember that this is still something that *supporters* of the law want, so it will be positive even though the clue is "as slowly as possible." "Get used to it" might be a good choice. "Revolt" is negative, so eliminate (B). Now look at (A) and (D): "implemented" (put into effect) makes sense, but "described" isn't something you do to a law, so eliminate (D). That leaves (A): logically, people who support a law would want it put into effect slowly so that people would have time to adapt.

2. A

The key phrase "spends little time describing their appearances" tells you that Kundera doesn't think his characters' appearances are very important. So you might try filling in something like "not very important." That is the definition of "peripheral" (PERI-, around, so something "peripheral" is on the edges), so (A) is correct. "Skeptical" (disbelieving), "reliant," "indispensible" (necessary), and "imbued" (full of) are unrelated to the sentence.

3. B

The sentence contrasts "consume more resources" with the first blank, so logically the word you want must mean "consumer *fewer* resources." "Delinquency" means "committing crimes," which doesn't fit. "Objectivity" (looking at things in an unbiased way) has nothing to do with resources. "Creativity" also doesn't fit. For the second blank, the clue is "conserve energy," which is an environmentally friendly action. So "responsible" would be a good word for the blank. Remember, though, that you've already crossed out (A). Someone "apathetic" is someone who doesn't care, so (D) is out. In choice (B), "sustainability" fits with consuming fewer resources, and being environmentally conscious works with conserving energy, so (B) is correct.

4. C

Since the researchers are making something look like something else, you can see that the words in the two blanks will be opposites. This lets you eliminate (A) because to do something in a "calculated" manner means to do it intentionally. In (B), "resolution" (firm decision) and "perceptive" have no relationship. (D) is also out, since a goal is not the opposite of "groundbreaking." "Complication" and "problematic" have similar meanings, so (E) can be eliminated as well. (C) fits because if researchers ignore their many failures and focus on their rare successes, their discoveries will appear much more deliberate rather than simply the result of chance (i.e. a fluke).

5. B

"Iron Lady" is a clue for both blanks, which must both mean something like "tough." For the first blank, "acquiescence" (giving in or agreeing) doesn't fit with tough, so cross off (C). For the second blank, "mercurial" (constantly changing, "conciliatory" (wanting to reconcile), and "cavalier" (offhand, not serious) don't fit with tough, so eliminate (A), (D), and (E). In choice (B), "obstinacy" (stubbornness) and "unyielding" (firm or stubborn) fit with the clue and are synonyms for each other, so (B) is correct.

Set 14 (p. 56)

1. B

The key phrase "deadliest and most economically destructive" indicates that the word in the blank must be negative and mean something like "really awful" or "disastrous." That is the definition of "catastrophic," so (B) is correct. The eruption may have been "stressful," "unexpected," and "continuous," but those words do not mean "disastrous," so (A), (D) and

(E) can be eliminated. In (C), "subtle" (understated) is the opposite of what you're looking for.

2. B

The construction "To _____, Lord North _____" tells you that the word in the second blank will be the result of the first. You can also make a reasonably educated guess that the first word will mean something like "calm" since governments don't usually try to make bad situations worse on purpose. Working on that assumption, you can eliminate (A) and (E) because "inflame" and "stimulate" are the opposite of what you're looking for, and (C) because "deny" is negative. Now look at the second blank: if the tariffs were rescinded (withdrawn), then logically the colonists would calm down, so (B) works. If, on the other hand, they were finalized, the colonists would probably get angrier, not be placated (calmed). So (D) can be eliminated. That leaves (B).

3. E

The key word "harshly" tells you that the director behaved poorly, so you're looking for two negative words. "Magnanimous" (MAGN-, big and ANIMUS, spirit) means "generous," so (A) doesn't work. "Compulsive" and "capricious" (unpredictable) also don't fit with behaving harshly, so eliminate (B) and (D). Now look at the second side. "Cajoled" (flattered, coerced) is positive, so eliminate (C). That leaves (E): the director would logically be considered "tyrannical" (cruel) if he harshly "berated" (criticized) the actors.

4. D

In the second half of the sentence, the idea that knowledge is the result of interactions with the physical world makes it clear that Locke thinks people are born without any knowledge to start with. So "inborn" or "pre-existing" would be good words for the first blank. "Definitive" (absolute) doesn't fit this clue; neither does "essential" (necessary), "tenuous" (just barely holding on), or "esoteric" (old and unusual). So without even looking at the second blank, you can eliminate all the answers but (D). Innate (IN- + NAT-, birth) means inborn, and derived fits with the second blank, so (D) is correct.

5. E

This sentence gives you two pieces of information to work from. The key phrase "defies any attempt at categorization" tells you that the second blank must mean something like "unique," and the word "while" at the beginning of the sentence tells you that the word in the first blank will mean the opposite of the second. Try filling in something like "boring" or "unoriginal." "Trite," "prosaic," and "hackneyed" all fit that definition, but (B) and (D) can be eliminated. Now look at the second side. "Platitudes" are clichés – that's the opposite of what you're looking for, so eliminate (A). "Innuendos" are subtle (critical) suggestions, which doesn't fit. That leaves (E): "idiosyncrasies" are eccentricities or particularities, which fits the idea of being unique.

Set 15 (p. 56)

1. C

The key word "confronted" is very oppositional, and tells you that these facts will somehow challenge the scientist's theory. Knowing this, you can plug in a word like "show" for the second blank. Only "demonstrate" and "reveal" are consistent with that idea, so you can eliminate (A), (D), and (E). Now look at the first side. The words "criticized" and "refusing" suggest that the scientists wanted to hold on to theory, even though it wasn't very good. But since the scientist has been criticized for *refusing* to _____, you're looking for a word that means "let go of." "Promote" is the opposite of "let go of," so eliminate (B). That leaves (C), which fits because "abandon" means "give up."

2. A

If people refer to the tomato as a vegetable even though it's actually a fruit, the name would be incorrect or inaccurate. "Panacea" means "cure-all," so (B) clearly doesn't fit. "Distraction" is tempting, but doesn't have the right connotation of inaccuracy. "Hypothesis" (guess) doesn't fit, and neither does "detriment" (damage, disadvantage). A misnomer (look at the root words MIS-, wrong, and NOM-, name) is an incorrect name, so (A) is the answer.

3. C

This sentence is a little tricky to figure out. From the first half, you can tell that the soil lacks nutrients, or is actually not very good for food production. However, it *looks* better than it is, because it has numerous trees and lush plant life. So the second blank probably describes how the European settlers thought the land had more potential for food production than it actually did. "Denying" doesn't make sense in this context, nor does "condemning" so (A) and (B) are out. "Contemplating" just means thinking about, which also doesn't have the idea of getting it wrong, so (D) is also out. There's nothing in the sentence to imply that the Europeans had to defend their views, so (E) doesn't fit the clues, either. That leaves (C). "Deceived" fits the clues about getting the wrong idea, and "overestimating" fits with the idea that the land looked better than it actually was.

4. C

Start with the second blank: "respect" is a clue telling you that the word will be positive, and "even" tells you the word will be similar in meaning to respect but more extreme. "Admiration" and "reverence" (deep admiration) fit, but "reticence" (reluctance), "remuneration" (compensation), and "perplexity" (confusion) don't, so eliminate (A), (D), and (E). The word "while" tells you that the first blank will mean the opposite of the second, so you're looking for a negative word.

"Chimerical" is a word that's often associate with monsters, but it means "imaginary," and sharks are very real, so eliminate (B). That leaves (C): "rapacious" means "ravenous" or "taking by force," so both words fit.

5. D

The colon indicates that the second half of the sentence will be explain the first part, so you know that "keen sense of observation" is a clue for the first blank, and "economy of expression" is a clue for the second. Start with the first blank since the second is likely to be less clear. "Keen sense of observation" is positive, so eliminate anything negative or unrelated to that description. "Descriptive" and "perspicacious" (perceptive) fit, but "unwavering" (standing firm), "ironic," and "bemusing" (puzzling) don't fit, so eliminate ((B), (C), and (E). Now look at the second side. "Economy of expression" means "not wordy," so the word you want must mean "not using a lot of words." That is the definition of "laconic," so (D) is correct. Careful not to get fooled by "prosaic:" although you might get tripped up because that word sounds similar to "prose," it means "unoriginal."

Set 16 (p. 57)

1. C

The key words "the new section" let you know that the lizard is repairing or re-growing the limb. "Regenerate" (RE-, again + generate, create) means "regrow," so (C) is correct. "Preserve" doesn't work since the lizard has already lost the tail. Eliminate (A). "Define," "strengthen," and "select" also don't have the idea of re-growing, so you can eliminate (B), (D) and (E) as well.

2. D

The sentence contrasts the blank with "rapidly mak[ing] many breakthroughs," so you're looking for a word that means the opposite. "Incremental" means "slow" or "a little bit at a time," so (D) fits the required definition.

"Experimental," "fortuitous" (occurring by chance) "collaborative" (working together), and "controversial" all do not fit.

3. E

"Preferred to spend his time alone" is a clue for both blanks. If the poet preferred to be alone, you could describe his personality as antisocial or something similar. "Aloof" (standoffish), "taciturn" (not talkative), and "misanthropic" (disliking people: MIS-, not + ANTHRO-, human) fit, but you can eliminate (A) and (C) "insufferable" (obnoxious) doesn't fit, and "flamboyant" (showy) is the opposite of what you want. Now look at the second side. If the poet liked to spend his time alone, he didn't like social gatherings, so you're looking for a negative word. "Mindful" is positive, so eliminate (A). "Defensive" doesn't fit – if the poet didn't like social gatherings, he wouldn't defend them. That leaves (E): "chary" means "suspicious," so (E) fits.

4. A

The word "although" tells you that the Incas' attempts to conquer northern Chile were unsuccessful. That information allows you to fill in something like "give up" for the first blank. "Resist" and "attack" are the opposite of what you want (remember, you're describing what the Mapuche *didn't* do), so cross off (B) and (C). "Exculpating" (freeing from guilt, EX-, from + CULP-, guilt) has nothing to do with giving up, so cross off (E) as well. If the Mapuche refused to give up, they did successfully resist. "Emancipating" means "freeing from slavery:" completely irrelevant. In choice (A), "capitulate" means "surrender," and "thwarting" means "preventing," so (A) is correct.

5. D

The key phrase "rewrote the ending…thirty-nine times" tells you that the word you want must have something to do with doing very careful work. "Equivocation" means wavering back and forth, which doesn't fit. "Stoicism" (not showing emotion), "punditry" (commenting on), and "discretion" (caution, politeness) also don't make sense in this blank. "Scrupulousness" means being very careful, and precedent means an example (note the prefix PRE-, before), so the correct answer is (D).

Set 17 (p. 58)

1. A

The construction "so many _____ accounts…that its exact appearance is a _____" tells you that the second blank must be a result of the first. In addition, the key word "extinct" tells you that no one today has seen a dodo bird, so logically no one knows exactly what it looked like. That tells you that the word in the second blank means something like "a mystery." Only (A) fits that definition, and the existence of "conflicting" (differing) accounts would cause no one to know what the dodo bird really looked like. "Template" (standard model), "debate," "curiosity," and "digression" (going off-topic) do not fit.

2. B

The key phrase "examine them closely and from multiple perspectives" tells you exactly what you need in the blank: you could even fill in "examine closely" for your own word. That is the definition of "scrutinize," so (B) is correct. "Gratify" (satisfy), "exonerate" (clear from guilt), "moderate," or "contrive" (think up) all do not fit.

3. D

Since the sentence is describing a disease, you know its effects will be negative and that you're probably looking for a word that means something like "destroy." For the first blank, "fertilize" is positive, so eliminate (A). For the second blank, "paragon" (example) and "balm" (soothing substance) are both positive, so eliminate (B) and (E). Now think about the meaning for (C) and (D). In (C), "corrupt" (debase one's morals) is negative, but it doesn't

mean "destroy," and citrus orchards don't have morals. In (D), "ravage" (thoroughly destroy) and "scourge" (something that causes a lot of trouble or suffering) are both negative and fit the sentence, so (D) is correct.

4. D

Start with the second blank. It's paired with "uninspired, " so you're looking for a negative word with a similar meaning. "Implicit" (implied), "erudite" (extremely learned), and "irrevocable" (unable to be taken back) don't fit, so eliminate (A)-(C). "Formulaic" and "pompous" (arrogant) are both negative, but "pompous" isn't a synonym for "uninspired," so (E) can be eliminated as well. "Formulaic" is a synonym for "uninspired," so (D) is correct.

5. B

Start with the second blank. Ingres is described as "profoundly respectful of the past," so the first blank will be positive. Eliminate (C) since "decried" is negative. The second blank is contrasted with "encroaching popularity of the *new* Romantic style," so the word must mean something like "traditional." "Intuition" (gut feeling), "provincialism" (narrow-mindedness), and "charlatanism" (fakery) all do not fit that idea. In (B), "orthodoxy" is established opinion or tradition. Someone profoundly respectful of the past would indeed "assume" (take on – note the second meaning) the responsibility of defending established opinion, so (B) is correct.

Set 18 (p. 58)

1. D

A drought should have a negative effect on the energy industry, so the first blank must be negative. "Improved" and "promoted" are positive, so eliminate (B) and (E). For the second blank, a lack of water would be damaging if the industry *needed* water, so fill in something like "needs." "Comply with" (obey) and "elaborate on" do not mean "need." "Depend on" fits for "need," so (D) is correct.

2. A

The key phrase is "more Olympic gold medals than any other female tennis player," which lets you know that you want a strongly positive word in the blank. "Indefensible" and "condescending" (looking down on) are negative. "Effusive" means "unreserved" or "enthusiastic" (e.g. an effusive greeting), so it doesn't fit the clue. "Benevolent" (look at the root BENE-, good, + VOL-, wish) means "well-wishing;" this is positive but doesn't match the clue. "Preeminent" means "most distinguished," which matches, so (A) is correct.

3. D

The key phrase is "seemingly contradictory goals." If roller coaster designers are to create successful rides, then they must "accomplish" or "bring together" these two goals. Even if you can't fill your own word, "successful" tells you that the word you're looking for is positive. "Reiterate" (repeat), "abolish" (get rid of), and "excoriate" (criticize harshly) all don't make sense, so eliminate (A), (C), and (E). "Ameliorate" (make better) is positive, but the roller coaster designers don't have to make their *goals* better, so (B) doesn't make sense either. "Reconcile" means "bring together," which fits the sentence exactly. You should be aware that "reconciling" two opposing ideas or beliefs is a common figure of speech, so when you see a sentence that clearly describes that idea, you should look for "reconcile" among the answer choices.

4. E

Icebergs, strong winds, and large waves are clues for the first blank; these are all dangerous to sailors, so try filling in "dangerous." "Placid" (peaceful, look at the root word PLAC-, peace), and "torpid" means "slow" or "lethargic," so (B) and (D) don't fit. For "voracious," look at the root word VORE-, eat (as in carnivore or herbivore): this doesn't make sense with the clue because icebergs don't eat anything, so (C) is also out. The word in the second blank will describe the sailors who actually try to go out in that kind of water: from the clues, it can mean "brave" or "stupid" or "crazy." "Incredulous" means "disbelieving" (look at the root words IN-, not, and CRED-, believe), which doesn't mean any of those things. "Foolhardy" (brave in a foolish way, note the word FOOL) makes sense as a description of sailors who venture out in perilous waters full of icebergs and waves, so (E) is correct.

5. E

The word "but" tells you that Tameka didn't take Alex's concerns very seriously, so try filling in "didn't worry" about or a similar word for the blank. "Evoked" (elicited, called forth) doesn't fit, and "bolstered" (supported) is the opposite of what you want, so cross off (B) and (C). For the second blank, if Tameka doesn't worry about his concerns, she thinks they're not important or silly, so you want a word that means something similar to that. "Anachronistic" (AN-, not, + CHRON-, time) means in the wrong time, so (A) doesn't fit. In (D), "impugned" (harshly criticized) contains the right idea, even if it doesn't sit quite comfortably in the sentence, but "litigious" (argumentative, quick to take legal action) doesn't fit at all. In choice (E), "dismissed" works for the first blank, and "immaterial" means "unimportant," so (E) is correct.

Set 19 (p. 59)

1. B

The sentence makes it clear that the "natural _____" fulfills the same function as vaccination, so you want a scientific word that means something like "protection." "Utility" (usefulness) doesn't fit; neither does "atrophy" (decay), "curiosity," or "infirmity" (illness). In choice (B), immunity does refer to protection from disease, so (B) is correct.

2. D

The word "but" tells you that there is a contrast between the blank and the fact that Mars "could have hosted microorganisms" in its early years, so the word in the blank must be negative as well as consistent with the idea that there is no more life on Mars. Try plugging in something like "bad for" or "unsuitable." (D) is correct because "inhospitable" means "unwelcoming" – if there isn't life on Mars, then clearly the planet doesn't welcome it. "Inapplicable" (can't be applied to), "endemic" (native) and "superfluous" (excessive) all do not fit the idea of not being suitable, so (A)-(C) can be eliminated. "Affirmative" is positive and is the opposite of what you're looking for, so (E) does not work either.

3. A

Start with the second blank since it's clearer than the first. If the managers took back something they had agreed to, the workers wouldn't be very happy with, so "_____on the contract" must describe a negative reaction. "Focused" and "depended" are positive, so cross off (B) and (C). "Ruminated" and "meditated" (thought deeply about) are also not negative enough, so eliminate (D) and (E). In (A), "stipulations" are the terms of a contract, which makes sense for the first blank, and to "renege on" is to go back on a decision, so (A) is correct.

4. C

The sentence contrasts differences in the brain with factors such as learning and practice. This tells you that the first word will mean something like "internal," while the second word will mean something like "outside" or "environmental." Start with the first blank. "Innate," intrinsic" and "structural" all fit, but you can eliminate (B) and (E). For the second blank, "congenital" (inborn) is the opposite of what you want, so eliminate (A), and "isolated" has nothing to do with being outside, so eliminate (D). That leaves (C). "External" is a good opposite for "intrinsic," so (C) is correct.

5. C

Start with the second blank since you have more information about it. The clue is "rapid," so you want a word that has to do with speed. "Abstruse" (abstract), "torpid" (slow), and "cloying" (overly sweet) don't fit, so eliminate (A), (B) and (D). Both "cursory" and "fleeting" are synonyms for "rapid," so look at the first blank. "Unhampered" means "unrestricted," so logically you need a word that means something like "heavy" or "large." "Cumbersome" (hard to manage) fits that definition perfectly, whereas "valuable" does not. So (C) is correct.

Set 20 (p. 59)

1. D

"One of 8,000" is a clue that the odds were very difficult. "Daunting" means "extraordinarily difficult to overcome," so (D) is correct. "Negligible" (unimportant), "impeccable" (perfectly done), "imaginary," and "captivating" all do not fit.

2. E

The sentence contrasts the old regime with the new Weimar Republic. Since the new republic does allow radical experimentation, you know the old regime did *not* allow it. So the word in the second blank must mean something like "forbidden." "Sacrificed" doesn't fit, and neither does "corroborated" (backed up) or "encouraged," so you can eliminate (B), (C), and (D). For the first blank, the abolition of censorship would logically lead to more experimentation, not less, so eliminate (A) because a dearth (lack) doesn't fit. In (E), an upsurge of radical experimentation would be a logical consequence of abolishing censorship, and "suppressed" is a good synonym for "forbidden," so (E) is correct.

3. E

Start with the second blank. "Rarely reconsiders once she has made up her mind" is the clue, so you're looking for a word that means something like "stubborn." "Forthright" (direct) doesn't fit, and neither does "astute" (clever), so eliminate (B) and (C). For the first blank, it's clear that the word will be the opposite of the second, so you want something to describe how Steven *does* reconsider. "Procrastinate" means "delay," and "speculate" means "guess," so eliminate (A) and (D). In (E), to vacillate is to waver, and steadfast means unchanging, so (E) is correct.

4. B

Here, the colon shows you the parallel structure between the two halves of the sentence, with the clue "provide momentary amusement" fitting the first blank, and "render lessons more vivid and memorable" fitting the second. Starting with the first blank, "quixotic" (absurdly idealistic) doesn't fit, so cross off (A). "Subtle" also doesn't work with the idea of amusement, and neither does "vital" (very important), so cross off (C) and (D). For the second blank, "stabilizing" has nothing to do with rendering lessons more vividly, so eliminate (E). "Didactic" (intended to teach) and "frivolous" (not serious) fits the blanks perfectly, so (B) is correct.

5. E

Since the candidate's predecessor angered the voters, it's logical that his policy was negative and that her promise would be to do something positive – so you're looking for a pair of opposites. Start by looking at the relationship between each pair of words. (A): "judiciousness" (wisdom, fairness) has nothing to do with "posterity" (left for future generations). (B): "coercion" is a synonym for "manipulation." (C): "naiveté" (innocence) has nothing whatsoever to do with "analysis." (D): "diffidence" (aloofness) has nothing to do with "emancipation" (liberation). That leaves (E): "profligacy" (wasteful spending) is precisely the opposite of "restraint," so (E) is correct.

Set 21 (p. 60)

1. B

The key words "Golden Age" indicate that the word in the blank must be positive, so you can immediately eliminate (C) and (D) because "declined" and "stagnated" are negative. "Mellowed" (became less strong) and "compounded" (combined different parts into a whole) don't make sense in context, so eliminate (A) and (E). "Flourished" means "thrived," which fits the idea of a Golden Age, so (B) is correct.

2. E

The clue for this blank is "thought to have originated," so "native" would be a good word to plug in the blank. "Associated with" is tempting, but this doesn't have the connotation of originating somewhere, so (A) doesn't fit. Same thing for "correlated with." "Subdued by" (repressed by) and "transferable to" don't work at all, so cross off (C) and (D). "Indigenous" means "native," so (E) is correct.

3. E

The sentence contrasts "familiar assumptions" with the blank, so you're looking for a word that means "unfamiliar." "Analogous" (similar) is the opposite of what you want, and "myopic" (narrow-minded, constrained), "uniform" (unvarying) and "trivial" (unimportant) all do not fit, so eliminate (A)-(D). "Alien" means "strange" or "foreign," so (E) is correct.

4. D

The sentence makes it clear that this was a moment of change: Napoleon's army changed from being invincible to being permanently damaged. Try filling in "critical" or "important" for the blank. A "watershed" moment is a critical moment or a turning point, so (D) is the answer. "Triumphal" (triumphant) is the opposite of what you want, and "resolute" (staunch, determined), and "conciliatory" (seeking to reconcile) don't fit, so eliminate (A)-(C). Careful with (E): "belligerent" (warlike, look at the root BELL-, war) is a tempting choice because the sentence is about a military invasion, but the word "because" tells you to focus on the permanent damage the army suffered, not on the fact that it invaded Russia, so (E) is also incorrect.

5. E

Work from the second blank since you have more information about it. The sentence contrasts the fact that the manuscript was originally thought to be a fraud with the fact that "experts _____ the author's identity," so you're looking for a word that means something like "confirmed." Only (B) and (E) fit that definition – "impugned" (harshly criticized), "alleviated" (lessened pain), and "foreseen" do not fit. Now think about the first blank: remember not to jump to (B) just because you know that the second side fits. The SAT will often provide more than one word with the same definition (or similar definition), and the correct answer will usually involve the harder version of the word. For the first blank, "negligibly" (unimportantly) doesn't fit – there's nothing in the sentence to suggest that the manuscript was not important, just that it was thought to be a fraud (and you can't assume one from the other). In (E), "ostensibly" (seemingly true) fits with the idea that experts were not sure of the author's identity, and "authenticated" fits for "confirmed."

6. E

Start with the first blank. "Failing spectacularly" is negative, so the first blank must be negative as well. "Acceleration" (speeding up) and "propagation" (increase, spreading; look at the prefix PRO-, in favor of, which is usually positive) are positive, so eliminate (A) and (D). Now look at the second blank. Potential for growth is good, so if a country *fails* by being unable to _____ that potential, the blank must mean something like "take advantage of."

"Revere" (deeply admire), "forestall" (prevent), "extirpate" (eradicate) and "unify" do not mean "take advantage of," leaving (E). "Tap" does indeed mean "take advantage of" (note the second meaning), so (E) is correct.

Set 22 (p. 61)

1. C

The key phrase "it had a major impact" indicates that the word in the blank must mean something like "important." "Influential" is most consistent with the meaning indicated by the sentence, so (C) is correct. All of the other answer choices involve words that are often *associated* with important books, but none actually fits the clue provided.

2. A

The key phrase "allegiance to the government" indicates that the word in the blank must mean something like "loyalty." That is the definition of "fidelity" (FID-, loyal), so (A) is correct. To eliminate judiciousness, think of the same root words in judicial and judge: this word means wisdom, which doesn't have to do with allegiance or loyalty. "Conscription" (being drafted into the military) has nothing to do with loyalty. For "subversion," you can take a clue from the prefix SUB-, underneath, to figure out that it's probably negative. "Subversion" means trying to overthrow the government, so it's the exact opposite of the word you want. "Equality" also has nothing to do with loyalty, so (E) is also wrong as well.

3. E

The construction "not only...but also" tells you that the two words will have related meanings, and that the word in the second blank will be a stronger version of the first. Think about the sentence logically for a moment: computers actually exist, so logically Turing probably showed how they could actually be built. (The SAT wouldn't try to "trick" you by making the correct answer something that wasn't true in the real world). The second blank should therefore be positive. "Ludicrous" (absurd) and "impractical" are negative, so eliminate (A) and (C). Since the two blanks must have similar meanings, the first blank will be positive as well. "Classified" is neutral and doesn't make sense in context, and "decried" (denounced) is negative, so eliminate (B) and (D). That leaves (E), which fits: "intuit" (have a gut feeling about) works in the first blank, and "feasible" (possible) works as a stronger version of the same idea, so (E) is correct.

4. D

For the first blank, the sentence contrasts "maximize the absorption" with "_____ the amount," so a word like "minimize" or "decrease" would be a good choice to fill in. "Stimulate" and "expand" are the opposite of this, so cross off (B) and (C). For the second blank, "avoid" gives you a clue about the word: it should have a similar meaning to the first blank. "Aggravate" (make worse) doesn't make sense, and "substantiate" (prove) also doesn't fit, so you can cross off (A) and (E). In choice (D), "moderate" is a good synonym for "minimize," and "mitigate" (look at the root MITI-, soft or gentle) means "make less bad," so (D) is correct.

5. A

Start with the second blank. The word "destructive" gives you a clue that the word will be strongly negative, so you can cross off (B), (C), and (E), because "edifying" (enlightening) "gratifying" (rewarding) and "astute" (smart) are positive. For the first blank, try filling in your own word: again, the key word "destructive" tells you the word will NOT be positive, but you'll run into trouble if you assume it has to be negative. You're left with (A) and (D), and "extolled" (praised) is strongly positive. This lets you cross off choice (D). In choice (A), "perceived" is neutral but makes sense in context, and "bankrupt" (devoid of any positive qualities) is strongly negative, so (A) is correct.

6. C

The negative key word "dismissed" lets you know that you're looking for a word in the second blank to describe a negative side of psychics and other mystical phenomena. Something like "nonsense" would be a good word to plug in. "Charlatanism" and "quackery" fit, so keep (A) and (C). "Impudence" (rudeness), "punditry" (being a public expert about a subject, e.g. a political pundit) and "coercion" (persuasion by force or threats) don't work, so eliminate (B), (D), and (E).
For the first blank, you're looking for a negative word to describe people who don't believe in psychics and other mystical phenomena. "Subdued" just means "lacking intensity," which doesn't have much to do with the clue. "Incredulous" means "disbelieving" or "skeptical," which is a strong fit for the clues about the colleagues, so (C) is correct.

Set 23 (p. 62)

1. B

The key phrase "present themselves in the best possible light" tells you that people will try to *hide* or *cover up* unflattering behaviors and experiences. To downplay is to make less noticeable, which fits with the idea covering something up, so (B) is correct. "Imitate," "endorse" (promote), and "resolve" do not fit, and "accentuate" (call attention to) is the opposite of the word you want.

2. C

The key words "only when" tell you that the cedars and teak trees were the first choice. So the architects would only turn to stone when the trees were unavailable. This lets you plug in "available" or something similar for the second blank. "Apprehended" means either "arrested" or "understood," and neither of those meanings fits here, so eliminate (A). (B) is out because "created" doesn't work (builders don't create trees). "Captured" also doesn't fit for trees, so cross off (E) as well. In choice (D), "intruded on" does not make sense when referring to stone, so (D) also doesn't work. In (C), "resorted to" works to describe using something as a second choice, and "obtained" fits the idea of availability, so (C) is correct.

3. D

Here, the Alps are high and imposing, but not quite a _____ barrier, so you know that the word in the first blank must be a stronger version of "high and imposing." "Unquestionable" clearly doesn't fit, and neither does "uncouth" (rude), so eliminate (A) and (E). "Inscrutable" (incomprehensible) also doesn't make sense, so eliminate (C). For the second blank, you can see that the second half of the sentence explains or gives more details about the first. "They were affirmed" by soldiers and merchants has nothing to do with whether or not the Alps were crossable, so (B) is out. In (D), "insurmountable" (uncrossable) is a more extreme version of "high and imposing," and "traversed" (crossed) fits for the second blank.

4. C

The structure "_____ by the _____" tells you that the second blank will be the result of the first. Either progress has been made because something good has happened to large-scale approaches, or progress has not been made because something bad has happened to large-scale approaches. The problem is that you have no way of knowing whether the two blanks will be positive or negative. So you're going to start by looking at just the relationship between each pair of words. (A): "accelerate" is positive but "destruction" is negative, so eliminate it. (B): "diminished" is negative, but "proliferation" (a large increase) is positive, so eliminate it. (C): "hindered" (prevented) is negative, as is "paucity" (small amount), so keep it. (D): "obstructed" is negative, but "popularity" is positive, so eliminate it. (E): "ameliorated" (improved, MELIOR-, better) is positive, but "dearth" (absence) is negative, so eliminate it. That leaves (C), which is the answer.

5. D

Start with the second blank. The key phrase "beyond a nationalist agenda" tells you that the word you're looking for must mean something like "international." "Universal" and "cosmopolitan" clearly fit, so keep (B) and (D). "Grandiose" might also seem plausible, so you can keep (C) as well. "Contemporary" (current) and "mellifluous" (sweet-sounding) don't fit at all, so eliminate (A) and (E). Now look at the first blank: if Glazunov "_____ his outlook *beyond* a national agenda," then logically this word must mean something like "expanded." "Restrained" and "*in*culcated" are both the opposite of what you want, so eliminate (B) and (C). "Broadened" fits perfectly, so (D) is correct.

6. D

The word "although" tells you that the words in the two blanks must have opposite meanings. Since the sentence is talking about "unexpected news," something that catches people off guard, you can also make a relatively educated guess that the word in the first blank will mean something like "unaffected," while the second blank will mean something like "affected." But start by looking at the relationship between each pair of words. (A): "irate" (angry) isn't the opposite of "bemused" (perplexed – careful, this word does NOT mean "amused"), and neither makes sense in context. (B): for the second blank, "flustered" (agitated, confused) fits, but it's not the opposite of "alert." (C): "stoic" (not showing emotion) works for the first blank, but it's a synonym for "unperturbed" (not bothered). (D): "composed" (calm) is the opposite of "nonplussed" (flustered), and those words make sense in context, so (D) fits. (E): "mesmerized" (fascinated) is a synonym for "engaged." So that leaves (D), which is the correct answer.

Set 24 (p. 62)

1. A

The key phrase "even people within the same city cannot agree on how they should be prepared" tells you that there are many different versions of these dishes. "Variations" captures the idea of many versions and makes sense in context: if there are many variations of a dish, then logically people would disagree about its preparation. "Descriptions," "flavors," "critics," and "ingredients" all do not capture the idea that the dish has many different versions.

2. B

In this sentence, the interaction between the grapefruit juice and the medications is described as dangerous. The two blanks are clearly contrasting (look at the key words "the difference between"), so if one is describing the dangerous interaction (negative), the other one must be positive. (A) looks tempting, but "reactive" doesn't work because this is a neutral word that could refer to either a good or a bad reaction. In (C), "prescriptive" looks tempting because it has to do with medicine, but remember that simply prescribing medicine is neither negative nor positive, so (C) doesn't work. (D) doesn't work because both words are negative; if you're stuck for "detrimental," look at the negative prefix DE-, and if you're stuck for "noxious," look at the root NOX-, harm. In (E), both "curative" and "salutary" (healthy) are positive, so eliminate it as well. In (B), "therapeutic" is positive and "toxic" is negative, so (B) is correct.

3. A

The sentence tells you that the painter's behavior was unpleasant, but it was _____ by others. The word "but" tells you that this will be a contrast, so you're looking for a word that indicates that there were no negative consequences for the unpleasant behavior. Try plugging something like "overlooked" or "allowed." "Abused" clearly doesn't fit, so (D) is out. "Chastised" means "scolded," so (E) also

doesn't work. For the second blank, his behavior would only be ignored because of his extraordinary abilities, so "dubious" (doubtful) doesn't fit. "Mundane" (commonplace) also doesn't fit with the idea of something exceptional, so cross off (C). In choice (A), "condoned" means "permitted," and "virtuosic" means "outstanding," so (A) is correct.

4. B

The key word "because" tells you that the second blank is the result of the first and that it must be similar to the idea of being "difficult to notice." Careful with the phrase "all but" – it means "essentially," and it's just there for emphasis. It has no effect on the meaning of the sentence, and if it confuses you, you can simply pretend it's not there. "Advantageous" (giving an advantage), "catastrophic" (disastrous) and "naturalistic" (seeming natural) have nothing to do with being difficult to notice. "Undeniable" is the exact opposite of the word you want. "Imperceptible" means "impossible to notice," which fits exactly, so (B) is correct.

5. E

The key words are "biting wit" – the word in the blank must have a similar meaning. "Timorous" (shy), "convoluted" (extremely complicated), "hackneyed" (unoriginal), and "florid" (flowery) all have nothing to do with biting wit, so you can eliminate (A)-(D). "Caustic" means "biting" or "extremely sarcastic" and fits perfectly, so (E) is correct.

6. E

The fact that the sentence is talking about vision *problems* tells you that the first blank will be negative: you can eliminate (A) and (C) because "rectified" (made right) and "complemented" (enhanced, made complete) are both positive. Now look at the second blank: the fact that O'Keefe worked until she was more than ninety years old tells you that you're looking for a positive word that means something like "continued." "Deviated" (went against) is negative, so eliminate (B). "Commemorated" (paid tribute to the memory of) is positive but does not fit at all with the idea of continuing on. In (E), "compromised" means "negatively affected" (note the second meaning), and "persevered" means "continued on."

Set 25 (p. 63)

1. A

The key word "banned" tells you that the word will have something to do with the games not being allowed. That is the definition of "prohibited," so (A) is correct. "Delay," "embellishment" (beautification), and "threat" all do not fit. Careful with (D): the Europeans did rebel by holding the Olympics, but the word in the blank refers to the ban, not the Europeans' action.

2. D

Even if you don't know anything about Kepler, the sentence suggests that he was a scientist and that he did something "correctly." What do scientists do? They *think up* theories. So you're looking for two relatively positive words that mean something like "think up." (A): "invent" is positive, but "refuting" is negative, so eliminate it. (B): "imagine" is positive, but "overturning" is negative, so eliminate it. (C): "disprove" is negative, so eliminate it. (D): "devise" (think up) and "formulating" are both positive, so keep it. (E): "develop" is positive, but "revoking" is negative, so eliminate it. That leaves only (D), which is correct.

3. B

The sentence contains a lot of information, so consider what you know before looking at the answers.

-The first half of the sentence tells you that reading has historically involved *only* the reader and the book.

-In the second half of the sentence, the key word "interactive" tells you that reading now involves more than just the reader and the book.

Therefore, reading is now *more* interactive – but the sentence expresses that idea the other way around (*less* _____). So you're looking for a word that means the *opposite* of interactive.

The only word that fits is "isolated:" if more elements than just the reader are involved in reading, then it *isn't* an isolated pursuit – by definition, a solitary activity is one that a person performs alone. "Comprehensive" and "collaborative" are the opposite of what you're looking for, so (A) and (D) don't work. "Intense" and "nostalgic" (longing for the past) simply make no sense in context, so (C) and (E) can be eliminated as well.

4. C

The key phrase "attempts at understanding" gives you a clue that these attempts were not successful, so try plugging in "stopped" or "prevented" for the second blank. "Confirmed" and "foretold" clearly don't work, so you can cross off (A) and (E). For the first blank, something that prevents an attempt at understanding would be a negative word like "problem." "Theorems" are theories, and "hypotheses" are guesses, which are neutral and don't mean "problem." In choice (C), "conundrums" are puzzles, and "stymied" means "prevented," so (C) is correct.

5. C

In this sentence, the key words "and indeed" tell you that the two blanks will be similar. The fact that the novelist studied anthropology suggests that that subject will have something to do with his work. You have a little more information about the second blank, so start with it. Try filling in "show up in" or "are found in." This lets you cross off (A) and (E), because "maintain" and "coddle" (pamper) don't make sense. For the first blank, if his works are full of anthropological references, than anthropology probably was important to them, so "challenged" and "demeaned" can't be right. Thus, (C) is correct. This is a difficult answer because "pepper" is more commonly used as a noun, but it can also be a verb meaning "sprinkle." But remember: second meanings are usually right, so when too-easy words show up as answers to hard questions, you need to consider that there might be an alternate meaning involved.

6. D

For the first blank, the key word is clear: you need something that fits with the concept of clarity. "Ingenuous" (naïve) and "supercilious" (condescending) don't fit, so eliminate (A) and (C). Now look at the second blank. Since the sentence praises the writer's work as "free of insider _____" you can also tell that the word in this blank will be negative. "Unequivocal" (clear, decisive) fits, but "admonition" (scolding) isn't its opposite, nor does it make sense in context, so eliminate (B). In (E), "precise" fits for the first blank, but "alacrity" (promptness, eagerness) is positive. In choice (D), "lucid" (look at the root LUC-, light) means clear, and "jargon" is insider language, so (D) is correct.

Set 26 (p. 64)

1. B

The key phrase "highly influential in the early women's movement" tells you that Mary Wollstonecraft had a positive attitude toward female equality. "Neglect" and "suspicion" are negative, so eliminate (C) and (D). Female equality also isn't something that can be "elected" or "detected," so eliminate (A) and E). "Advocacy" (promotion) fits with the idea of someone highly influential in the women's movement, so (B) is correct.

2. B

The Joshua trees are described as an indicator species, implying that they're the plants that define the boundaries of the Mojave. So fill in

"defined" or a similar word in the blank. "Integrated," "standardized," "challenged," and "polarized" (divided into opposing groups) don't fit here, but "demarcated (marked out or defined) does," so (B) is correct.

3. B

The word in the blank must describe someone in an authoritarian regime who wants democratic reform. Authoritarian governments don't support democracy, so you want a word for someone who opposes the government. The only word that fits the idea of opposing the government is (B) because dissidents (look at the prefix DIS-) are opponents of a regime or an ideology. "Ambassadors," "loyalists," "denizens" (residents), and "mercenaries" (soldiers for hire) all have nothing to do with political opposition.

4. C

In this sentence, the construction "not only _____ but also _____" sets up a parallel between "false memories" and the word in the blank, telling you that it must mean something similar to "false." That is the definition of "spurious," so (C) is correct. "Inconsistent," "elaborate" (detailed and complex), "diabolical" (evil), and "cerebral" (having to do with the brain, or involving intellect rather than emotions) all do not mean "false." Be careful with (B) and (E): the memories created by the researchers *could* be elaborate, but the sentence is telling you that the word you want *must* mean "false." Same for "cerebral:" if the recollections are being generated in the brain, then they are technically cerebral, but again, that's not the definition the sentence indicates the correct word must have.

5. D

If "*no* known civilization has _____" solitary living as a social ideal, then most people are probably not going to react positively to the idea that people who live alone are happier than those who don't. So logically, the first blank must mean something like "doubt" or "surprise." If you plugged in "skepticism," don't automatically choose (B) – you have to consider all the answers that have similar meanings. Both "disbelief" and "derision" could fit as well. You can, however, cross off (C) and (E) because "contemplation" (deep thought) and "elation" (joy) do not fit.

Now look at the second side: logically, people would reject the idea that living alone makes you happy if every civilization has *rejected* living alone. But wait: the negation *no* known civilization tells you that the word itself has to be positive. "Abhorred" (loathed) and "repudiated" (strongly rejected) are negative, so eliminate (A) and (B). That leaves (D): "derision" means "looking down on," and "touted" means "praised," which both fit the sentence.

6. D

The key phrase "even foreboding" tells you that the word in the first blank is similar in meaning to "foreboding" but less extreme. "Imposing," "austere," and "grave" (serious) all fit, but "eccentric" (odd) and "jovial" (cheerful) don't, so eliminate (A) and (C). Now look at the second side. "Belied" means "contradicted," so you're looking for the opposite of "foreboding." "Condescending" (looking down on) is similar, so eliminate (B), and "authoritarian" is similar as well, so eliminate (E). That leaves (D): "ebullient" means "enthusiastic and outgoing," so both words fit.

Set 27 (p. 65)

1. D

"Deafen" is strongly negative; however, the word "but" implies that whales can do something to make the negative consequences less severe by blocking their ears. Try filling in "lessen" or "help stop" for the blank. "Lament" (be sad about), "reveal" and "reciprocate" (give in return) don't match the clue, and "intensify" is the opposite of what you want. "Alleviate" means "make less bad," so (D) is the answer.

2. C

The key words "overdevelopment" and "problem" tell you that the word in the first blank is going to be negative, so eliminate (A) and (D) because "integration" and "restoration" are clearly positive. "Dilution" (making less strong by adding more liquid) also doesn't make sense, so eliminate (B). Now look at the second side. "Denied" doesn't make any sense because marine biologists would want people to know about the problem, so eliminate (E). "Highlighted" does make sense because logically, if the marine biologists are at an environmental summit, they're going to want to call attention to the problem. So (C) is correct.

3. E

The construction "so _____ that _____" tells you that the second blank is the *result* of the first. Since the sentence offers no clues about what the two words might mean, focus on the relationship between the words in each pair of answers. (A) may be tempting, but composers would not automatically be moved by musical styles just because they were popular. "Melodious" (nice-sounding) styles would not cause composers to become deluded, so eliminate (B). A style becoming "outdated" would not cause composers to become affected – it would have the opposite effect, so eliminate (C). A style becoming "cacophonous" (harsh-sounding) would not make composers enervated (tired and weak), so eliminate (D). In choice (E), styles that were "ubiquitous" (everywhere) would cause composers to be influenced by them, so (E) is correct.

4. C

In this sentence, it's clear that you want opposite words for the blanks, since it's a before/after contrast. In (A), "outlawed" and "denounced" (criticized) are too similar, almost synonyms. In (B), "condoned" is a synonym for "allowed." In (D), "accepted" has no relationship to "discerned" (identified). In (E), a practice can't really be misplaced. Besides, "misplaced" and "permitted" have no relationship to one another. In (C), "prohibited" means made illegal, while "sanctioned" means allowed, so (C) is correct. Note that "sanction" has two contradictory meanings: as a noun, a sanction is a prohibition; as a verb, "sanction" means "permit."

5. C

The key phrase is "fear that speaking out," which indicates that the correct word will have something to do with staying silent. "Tacitly" means "silently," so (C) is correct. "Irrevocably" (permanently), "remotely" (from a distance), and "indignantly" (angrily, feeling insulted) do not fit the clue, so (A), (B) and (E) can be eliminated. "Vociferously" (loudly, VOC-, voice) is the opposite of what you want, so (D) can be eliminated as well.

6. B

This sentence draws a clear contrast between the first blank and the second. The clue for the second blank is "lasted seven years and involved numerous revisions," so "long-term" or a similar word would be good to plug in. In choice (A), "verifiable" (VER-, truth) means "provable," which has nothing to do with taking a long time, so cross off (A) – it doesn't matter that "hasty" fits for the first blank. In (C), "haphazard" means "careless," more of an antonym than a synonym for the word you want. Then look at the first blank. Since it's a direct opposite of the second, it will mean something like "quick." "Meticulous" (highly detailed) is the opposite of what you want, so eliminate (D). "Dexterous" (flexible) doesn't fit at all, so eliminate (E). That leaves (B): "cursory" means "done quickly," and "protracted" means "lengthy," which both fit.

Set 28 (p. 65)

1. C

The key word is "unfamiliar." The sentence is saying that all living creatures seek *new* things, so the word in the blank must mean something like "new." If you don't know what "novelty" means, look at the root word NOV-, new. That can give you the answer immediately. Otherwise, "repentance" is being sorry for something bad that you did, which doesn't work. "Modesty," "solitude" (being alone, think of SOL-, alone), and curiosity also don't match the idea of newness. Be careful with (E), though: although the sentence suggests that all living creatures *are* curious, they are not *seeking* something curious.

2. C

The key word "fakers" tells that the word in the blank must mean "making up" or "faking." That is the definition of "fabricating," so (C) is correct. "Describing," "venerating" (deeply respecting), "tolerating," and "supplying" all do not mean "faking."

3. D

The sentence establishes a contrast between the way Greek myths were "originally _____" and how they are "transmitted" today, so you're looking for a synonym for "transmitted." "Disseminated" (spread) fits that definition, so (D) is correct. "Contained," "identified," "analyzed," and "dispelled" (made to go away) all do not fit.

4. B

The phrase "bold optimist" tells you that Rivera had a positive attitude toward the revolution. "Decried" (denounced) and "vituperated" (harshly criticized) are negative, so eliminate (C) and (E). In addition, "stipulated" (required, demanded) isn't positive either, so eliminate (D). Now look at the second blank. You need a somewhat negative word that contrasts with the word in the first blank. "Enthusiastic" is positive, so eliminate (A). That leaves (B): "extolled" (praised) fits, and "apprehensive" (nervous) provides the necessary contrast.

5. A

The key phrase "an outdated relic of a pre-technological" age tells you that you're looking for a word that means something like "outdated." That is the definition of "anachronism" (ANA-, not + CHRON-, time), so (A) is correct. "Conversion" (change), "omen" (sign or warning about a future event), "abatement" (subsiding), and "paradigm" (standard model) all do not fit.

6. E

The key words "perceive miniscule distinctions" tell you that the word in the blank must mean "able to perceive miniscule distinctions." That is the definition of "discriminating" (note the second meaning), so (E) is correct. "Lugubrious" (sad), "munificent" (generous), "prescient" (knowing something before it happens), and "voluptuous" (sensually gratifying) all do not fit.

Set 29 (p. 66)

1. D

The key words "no more living speakers" let you know what to look for in this blank. Try filling in "dead" or something similar. "Extinct" fits that definition, so (D) is correct. "Colloquial" (casual language), "exotic," "dialect" (regional form of a language), and "indigenous" (native) all do not fit.

2. C

The key words "pioneer in the business" tell you that you're looking for a word about a groundbreaking businessman. An outcast doesn't fit, so eliminate (A). Be careful with (B) and (D): Mozart was both a virtuoso and a prodigy (both words mean someone very skilled at something), but that's not what the clue is

asking for, so don't be tempted by these false choices. An altruist is someone who does good works, so (E) is also out. An entrepreneur is someone who creates their own business opportunities, so (C) is correct.

3. D

Work from the second blank. The strongest key words in the sentence are "compelling new evidence," and they indicate that the second blank must be positive. Try filling in something like "prove." You can also fill in something like "proven" for the first blank. Now look at the answers, but make sure you don't jump to pick (C) just because the second side obviously fits. "Mitigate" means "lessen" or "reduce the severity of," and that clearly has nothing to do with proving. In (B), "upheld" works as a synonym for "prove," but "initiate" means "begin," which doesn't fit. (D) is the only other answer choice that works for the second side – "substantiate" means "prove," and "vindicate" (uphold with evidence) works as well, so (D) is correct.

4. A

The key phrase "fixed and universal" tells you about the blank: since the sentence draws a contrast between the blank and these words, you want a word for the blank that means something like "unsettled" or "individual." That's not what "vivid" (bright, striking) means, so eliminate (C). "Esoteric" means "obscure," which also doesn't work. Immutable (IM-, not, + MUT-, change) is the opposite of what you want, and "antiquated" (old, think of an antique) doesn't work either. You might only be familiar with "elastic" as a noun, but it can also be an adjective describing something changeable. Thus, (A) is correct.

5. E

The key phrase "never took his art seriously" tell you that you're looking for a word that means something like "amateur." A "prevaricator" is a liar, so (A) is out. Break down "contemporary" into CON-, with and TEMP-, time: a contemporary is someone who lives at the same time as someone else, so (B) doesn't fit either. An "aesthete" is someone who loves beauty, but that has nothing to do with not taking art seriously enough to pursue it professionally, so eliminate (D). A "usurper" is someone who unfairly forces their way into power, so (C) is also wrong. A "dilettante" is someone only superficially interested in something, so (E) is correct.

6. D

Here, the parallel structure of the sentence ("both _____ and _____") defines both words for you: the first blank will mean "excessively sentimental," and the second will mean "lacking psychological depth." For the first blank, "maudlin," "cloying," and "mawkish" all mean "excessively sentimental," but you can eliminate (C) and (E) because "bellicose" (aggressive) and "erudite" (extremely learned) don't fit. For the second blank, "profane" (vulgar, disrespectful of a something holy) doesn't work so eliminate (A), and "incidental" (unimportant) doesn't work, so eliminate (B). That leaves "superficial," which does mean "lacking psychological depth," so (D) is correct.

Set 30 (p. 67)

1. B

The key phrase "help harvest rain" lets you know that this blank will be a positive word. Try plugging in "improved" or "helped." "Enhanced" (improved) fits, so (B) is correct. "Disabled" is the opposite of what you're looking for, so eliminate (A). And although "consumed" (ate), "fertilized," and "marketed" are all words related to food and food production, none of them fits the clue.

2. D

The phrase "countless hours as well as vast sums of money to combatting poverty and other social ills" lets you know that the word in the

first blank will describe a generous person and that the word in the second blank will be positive. A philanthropist (PHIL-, love, + ANTHRO-, human) is a person who donates their money to good causes, and "devoted" is consistent with that idea as well, so (D) is correct. In (A), "altruist" (do-gooder) fits for the first blank, but "deported" is negative and doesn't fit. "Collaborator" (CO-, with + LABOR-, work) is someone who works with someone else, so (B) also doesn't fit. An impersonator is someone who imitates other people, so (C) doesn't work, and a traitor is someone who commits a betrayal, so (E) is incorrect.

3. A

The key phrases "little or no damage" and "rarely becoming invasive" indicate that the word in the blank must be neutral/positive and mean something like "harmless." If you don't know what "innocuous" means, skip it. (C) and (D) can be eliminated immediately because "aggressive" and "invasive" are clearly negative. "Organic" and "biological" are both related to plants, but they don't mean "harmless." That leaves you with (A), and in fact, "innocuous" does mean "harmless" (IN-, not + NOC-, harm).

4. D

The key words "require clear answers" tell you about the blank: since her friends *avoid* asking her these questions, you know that Alison is someone who has trouble giving clear answers. That means you're looking for a word that means something like "be unclear." That is the definition of "equivocate," so (D) is correct. "Rationalize" (justify), "dawdle" (delay), "acquiesce" (give in), and "prevaricate" (lie) all do not fit.

5. B

The key word "despite" tells you that the two words will have opposite meanings. Since the sentence gives you no information about the meaning of either word, start by looking at the relationship between each pair of words. (A): "equanimity" (ability to stay calm under stress) isn't the opposite of "eminent" (well-known). (B): "befuddlement" (confusion) is the opposite of "astute" (sharp, perceptive). (C): "geniality" (friendliness, happiness) is a synonym for "joviality." (D): "skepticism" (disbelief) isn't the opposite of "magnanimous" (very generous). (E): "haplessness" (having bad things *happen* to you) isn't the opposite of "partisan" (adhering strongly to a political party or group). (B) is the only answer that contains a pair of opposites, so it is correct.

6. D

The fact that more than 2,000 neologisms (new words – NEO-, new + LOGO-, word) are found in Shakespeare's writing tells you that Shakespeare enjoyed creating new words. Try filling in something like "created" for the second blank: "theorizing," "impugning" (strongly criticizing), and "eschewing" (rejecting) all do not fit, so eliminate (A), (B), and (E). Now look at the first side: if Shakespeare liked creating new words, then you know you're looking for something positive. "Abhorrence" (loathing) is negative, leaving (D). A propensity is an inclination toward something, and "coining" means "inventing" (note the second meaning).

Set 31 (p. 68)

1. A

Since we're also talking about dinosaur *enthusiasts*, we can also assume that the first blank will be relatively positive. "Distasteful" and "confined" (restricted) are negative, so eliminate (C) and (E). The key words "because of" immediately let you know that the second word will be the cause of the first. "Distinctive" (unique) fits because distinctive plates would make the stegosaurus easy to identify (identifiable), so (A) is correct. "Enervating" (tiring, weakening) and "assiduous" (hardworking) do not make sense in context.

2. C

The key phrase "it is often *helpful* to read several books about the same topic" tells you that the word in the first blank will probably be a positive/neutral word that means something like "explain" or "discuss," and the word in the second blank will probably be a negative word that means "don't include." Start with the second blank since there are fewer possibilities for what the word can mean: "overlook" and "neglect" fit, but you can eliminate (A), (D), and (E). Now look at the first blank. "Alienate" (exclude) is negative, so eliminate (B). That leaves (C): "illuminate" means "shed light on," which is consistent with the idea of explaining, and "neglect" is consistent with the idea of not including.

3. B

The key phrase "the Mughal Empire's *golden age*" tells you that the sentence is talking about the best period in the empire's history, so logically artistic and architectural production must have reached their highest point then. "Zenith" means "high point," so (B) is correct. "Abeyance" (cessation), "consensus" (agreement), "objective" (goal), and "conclusion" all do not fit.

4. A

The key words "reveled" and "arguing unpopular positions" tells you that you're looking for a word that describes someone who enjoys going against the norm. That is the definition of "contrarianism" (CONTR-, against), so (A) is correct. "Adulation" (adoration), "pacifism" (promoting peace), "hubris" (extreme arrogance), and "whimsy" (playfulness) all do not fit.

5. D

Start with the second blank since you have more information about it. The sentence contrasts the "suspected…damage" with the reality that the wings "were in fact _____," so the blank must mean something like "undamaged." "Deficient" (look at the negative prefix DE-) is the opposite of the word you want, so eliminate (A). "Treacherous" (dangerous) also conveys the opposite idea, so eliminate (C). Inanimate objects cannot be "resolute" (determined), so eliminate (E). Moving on to the first blank, try filling in "underwent" or something similar. "Suspended" doesn't fit, so (B) is out. That leaves (D): "sustained" means "underwent," and "sound" means "in good working order" (note the second meaning), so (D) is correct.

6. A

The sentence sets up a contrast between the two blanks but gives you no information about the definition of either word, so start by looking at the relationship between each pair of words. (A): "reticent" (reserved) is the opposite of "loquacious" (talkative), so (A) fits. If you're not comfortable picking it, look at the rest of the answers. (B): "ostentatious" (showy) isn't the opposite of "candid" (direct). (C): "Laconic" (not talkative) is similar to "diffident" (aloof). (D): "garrulous" (talkative, outgoing) has nothing to do with "impetuous" (unpredictable). (E): "defensive" isn't the opposite of "obstreperous" (loud and noisy).

Set 32 (p. 68)

1. E

The sentence tells you that the second blank is the result of the first, so you're either looking for two positive or two negative words. "Efficiency" is positive, but "denounced" is negative, so eliminate (A). "Consequences" is neutral, but "corrupted" is negative and makes no sense in context, so eliminate (B). "Benefits" is positive, but "mocked" is negative, so eliminate (C). "Value" is positive, but "questioned" is negative,

so eliminate (D). Both "inadequacy" and "vetoed" are negative and make sense in context (if the plan wasn't any good, then obviously the city council members would reject it), so (E) is correct.

2. D

In this sentence, bell hooks is the name that Gloria Watkins used as a writer, so fill in pen name or something similar for the blank. "Inspiration" doesn't match; neither does "acclaim" (praise), "perseverance" (persistence), or "anecdotes" (short stories). Be careful with (E): even though anecdotes are related to writing, the word doesn't fit the clue, so it isn't the correct answer. In (B), the root word PSEUD-, false + -NYM, name, is your clue that this is the answer; a pseudonym is a pen name or an alias.

3. A

The key word "however" tells you that the words in the two blanks will have opposite meanings. (A) is correct because "impede" (prevent) is the opposite of "enhance" (improve). In (B), "augment" (increase) and "stimulate" (provoke, elicit) have similar meanings. In (C), "obstruct" (get in the way of) has no relationship to "analyze." In (D), "inhibit" (prevent) is a synonym for "hinder." And in (E), "symbolize" has no relationship to "amplify" (make bigger or more extreme), and neither word fits.

4. C

Start with the second blank since it's a bit more straightforward. The sentence is talking about employers who *refuse* to let workers telecommute from home, so logically, they'd be concerned about their ability to figure out their workers' productivity. That means you're looking for a word that means something like "figure out." "Exacerbate" means "make worse," and "mitigate" means "lessen something bad," neither of which fits, so eliminate (A) and (D).

Now look at the first blank. If workers are telecommuting from home, that means they're far away. So you're looking for a word consistent with the idea of being far away. "Experience" has nothing to do with being far away, so eliminate (B).

Now be very careful with (E): you must separate the *idea* that the sentence is expressing from the actual word you're looking for. The idea that the sentence needs to convey is that workers are far away; however, the phrase "*lack* of _____" tells you that you're looking for a word that means the opposite of "far away," i.e. "nearness." So "distance" is the opposite of what you're looking for, meaning that you can eliminate (E). That leaves (C): "proximity" means "nearness," and "ascertain" means "figure out" or "determine" (literally, become certain about), so (C) fits.

5. B

The key word "thus" tells you that the word in the second blank will be the result of the first. In addition, if television viewers can't judge the _____ of the plots, they lack knowledge about technology, so trying plugging in a positive word like "knowledge" for the first blank. Unfortunately, "susceptibility" (vulnerability) is the only somewhat negative word, but you can at least eliminate (C). Now look at the second blank. If TV viewers don't know about technology, they can't judge how accurate the plots are, so plug in something like "accuracy" for the second blank. "Propriety" (proper behavior), "propensity" (liking for, tendency toward), and "gravity" (seriousness) all do not fit, so eliminate (A), (D), and (E). In (B), "veracity" means "truthfulness" (VER-, truth) which makes sense, and "acumen," means "smarts," which also fits as a synonym for "knowledge."

6. A

Start with the second blank since you have a lot more information about it. The fact that "no reputable publishing company" would take on

"Howl" tells you that the word in the second blank has to be negative. "Canonical" (conforming to an accepted form or tradition) and "revered" (deeply admired) are both positive, so eliminate (B) and (D). In addition, "quixotic" (absurdly idealistic) also doesn't quite fit with the idea of no reputable publishing house wanting to accept Ginsberg, so you can make an educated guess that (E) is probably wrong as well. Now look at the first side. The construction "_____ made him a _____" figure tells you that the word in the first blank was the cause of the second. Writing about "arcane" (highly specialized, difficult to understand) subjects wouldn't automatically make someone controversial, so (C) doesn't fit. In (A), writing about "taboo" (inappropriate, unacceptable) subjects would logically make Ginsberg a "polemical" (divisive) figure, so (A) is correct.

Set 33 (p. 69)

1. C

The information after the colon parallels the two blanks, providing the definition for each. The word in the first blank corresponds to "makes certain to finish each task completely," and the second word corresponds to "pays great attention to detail." Only "thorough" corresponds to finishing each task completely, and "meticulous" (precise) corresponds to paying attention to detail, so (C) is correct. The only other option that fits for the second blank is "careful," and "lackadaisical" means "lazy," which is the opposite of what is required for the first blank.

2. E

The list of countries tells you that Noguchi's work is influenced by many different styles and traditions, so you're looking for something that means "varied" or "diverse." That is the definition of "multifarious," so (E) is correct. Even if you're not familiar with this word, the prefix MULTI- (many) should give you a big clue that it's the answer. "Contiguous" (connected) does not fit at all, and "accessible," "realistic" and "appealing" are all words that *could* describe sculptures but that don't have the meaning that the sentence requires.

3. B

The sentence contrasts "terrestrial" (land-dwelling) with the blank, so you want a word that means the opposite of "terrestrial." In addition, the phrase "possess adaptations for climbing trees" tells you that the word you want must be related to trees. "Arboreal" (relating to trees, ARBOR-, tree) fits that definition, so (B) is correct. "Omnivorous" (eating everything, OMNI-, all + VOR-, devour), "predatory" (hunting) "aquatic" (water-dwelling), and "nomadic" (wandering) all do not fit.

4. D

The fact that a comparable snowstorm had not occurred in the springtime for a century indicates that you're looking for a word that means "unusual." That is the definition of "exceptional" (literally "an exception," i.e. "not the norm"), so (D) is correct. "Interminable" (endless), "enthralling" (thrilling, fascinating), "imminent" (about to happen), and "rousing" (emotionally stirring) all do not fit.

5. E

The key phrase "only the information necessary to form a coherent whole" tells you that the brain must not make use of all the information it receives. So the word in the first blank is negative and means something like "gets rid of." That eliminates (B) and (C) because "enhances" and "invigorates" (energizes) are positive. Now look at the second blank: it must be a positive word meaning something like "holding onto." "Proliferating" is positive, but it means "increasing" or "multiplying," which doesn't fit, so eliminate (A). "Discarding" is negative, so you can eliminate (D), leaving (E). "Eschews" means "rejects," and "retaining" means "holding onto," so (E) fits.

6. D

The key words "while" and "reality" tell you that there will be a contrast between "empathy and compassion" and the second blank. "Erudition" (deep knowledge), "apprehension" (nervousness), and "conjecture" (guesswork) all do not fit, so eliminate (A), (C), and (E). "Opprobrium" (disgrace, contempt) and "diffidence" (aloofness, lack of concern) are both possible as the opposite of "empathy and compassion." Now look at the first blank. Medical training is clearly going to have a positive relationship to "empathy and compassion." "Eschews" (rejects) makes no sense in context: medical training does not formally reject empathy and compassion. That leaves (D): "espouses" means "promotes," so (D) fits.

Set 34 (p. 70)

1. B

The sentence draws a contrast between "*similar* appearances and _____ traits," so the word in the blank should mean something like "different." "Unexpected," "striking," and "aggressive" (prone to attack) all don't fit, and "common" is exactly the opposite of what you're looking for. "Divergent" (look at the prefix DI-, apart) fits as a synonym for "different," so (B) is correct.

2. C

If the louse destroyed thousands of vineyards, people would be attempting to get rid of it, so "destroy" or "wipe out" would be good to plug in for the blank. "Amplify" means make bigger, which doesn't fit, so eliminate (B), and alleviate (look at the root LEV-, lift) means to make a problem less bad so (E) is also out. The sentence draws a contrast (but) between the first and the second blank: although people have tried to wipe out the louse, it has survived anyway. "Good at" would be a good plug-in for the second blank. Careful with (A): the louse is "resistant to" *being destroyed*, not "resistant to" *surviving*, so this answer creates a meaning that's exactly the opposite of what you want. In (D), "challenged by" simply doesn't make sense. In (C), "eradicate" (look at the roots E-, out from, and RAD-, root) means wipe out, and "adept at" means skilled at, so (C) is correct.

3. A

The key words "blend" elements tell you that the word in the blank will have something to do with mixing or blending. Something "syncretic" blends two opposing things (think of "in sync," together), so (A) is correct. "Recondite" (esoteric, obscure), "pedestrian" (unoriginal), "invaluable" (priceless), and "objectionable" are all unrelated to blending, so (B)-(E) can be eliminated.

4. D

Start with the second blank. The phrase "amending (added to) their own ideas accordingly" tells you that these scholars pay attention to information that contradicts their interpretations, so the second blank must be positive. "Annihilate" (completely destroy) and "stifle" (suppress) are clearly negative, so eliminate (A) and (C). Now look at the first blank: the phrase "but rather" tells you that it must mean the opposite of the first – try filling in something like "ignore." "Publicize" clearly doesn't work, so eliminate (B). Careful with (E) – don't just jump to pick it because you see "ignore." The first side obviously fits, but look at the second: "implicate" means "show that someone is involved in an event, often a crime," which has nothing to do with what the sentence is saying. That leaves (D), and "acknowledge" fits the sentence.

5. B

The fact that Tesla resigned from his job indicates that he had a negative attitude about it. For the first blank, try filling in a negative word like "unhappy." For the second, you can assume that he was unhappy because he had received *in*sufficient amounts of something good, like

praise – so the second blank will be positive. For the first blank, you can eliminate (A) since "exultant" means "overjoyed." Now look at the second blank. "Accolades" fits, so keep (B). "Exemptions" (excusals from unpleasant tasks) is somewhat positive but doesn't make sense in context, so eliminate (C). And "caveats" (warnings) and "demerits" (marks indicating bad behavior) are negative, so eliminate (D) and (E). That leaves (B), which is correct. Tesla would logically be "indignant" (angry, insulted) if he believed that his contributions hadn't received enough praise.

6. A

The key word "because" at the beginning of the sentence tells you that the second blank will be the result of the first. The information that "Shayla could only _____ the true motives behind her dismissal" suggests that her supervisor refused to tell her why she was fired, so try plugging in something like "tell her" for the first blank and "guess" for the second. For the first blank, "enumerate" (list), "disclose" (reveal), and "elucidate" (clarify) all work, but "exculpate" (free from blame, EX-, from + CULP-, guilt) and "peruse" (examine closely) don't fit, so eliminate (D) and (E). Now look at the second blank. "Surmise" means "guess" or "assume," so (A) works, but "determine" and "substantiate" (prove) are the opposite of what you're looking for – the whole point is that Shayna didn't know for sure. (B) and (C) can thus be eliminated, leaving (A).

Set 35 (p. 71)

1. A

The second half of the sentence defines the blank, so you're looking for a word that means "contrasting images placed next to one another." A juxtaposition is a display of two contrasting things side by side, so (A) is correct. "Symbols," "motifs," "illustrations," and "representations" are all things associated with paintings but do not refer to contrasting images.

2. D

The sentence contrasts a *single* protein with *several* different proteins working in _____, telling you that you want a word that has to do with working together. "In tandem" means "together," so (D) is correct. "Defense," "reaction," "vain" (without success), and "advance" all do not fit.

3. C

If the sailors knew to stop and get water at the Carioca River, it must have been well-known or famous for its pristine water. Even if you're not sure of the second blank, you can assume that the first blank will be a positive word meaning something like "famous." Looking at *only* the first blank, you can cross off every answer except (A) and (C). Look at DIS- in "disdained" and VILE in "reviled" to make an educated guess that these two words are negative and don't fit. Now look at the second blank. If the river was famous, then obviously sailors would like its water, so you're looking for a positive word here as well. "Discard" (throw away) is negative, so eliminate (A). That leaves (C): "renowned" fits for "famous," and "replenish" means "refill," which makes perfect sense in context.

4. E

The key phrase "purely by chance" tells you that you're looking for a word that means "by chance." "Infelicitous" means "unlucky" (IN-, not + FELIX-, luck) so cross off (A). In (B), the root CHRON-, time, should tell you what this word means: chronology has nothing to do with chance. "Specious" means "false," so (C) doesn't fit either. Choice (D) might be tempting because "astronomical" has to do with comets, but that's not what the clue is hinting at, so cross it out. "Serendipitous" means "lucky," so (E) is correct.

5. C

The key word "because" at the beginning of the sentence tells you that the second blank will be the result of the first. Since the sentence gives you no direct information about the meaning of either blank, start by considering the relationship between each pair of words. (A): if the compound inhibited (prevented) the onset of the disease, that would make it easier to find a treatment, so the researchers would be happy, not "dubious" (doubting). (B) has the same problem as (A). If the compound "thwarted" (prevented) the onset of the disease, then researchers would be inclined to believe that a new treatment could be developed, but "bemused" (puzzled) is negative. In (D), "permeate" (penetrate) simply makes no sense: a compound can't penetrate a *disease*. In (E), "forestall" (prevent) works, but "incensed" (angered) makes no sense. That leaves (C): if the compound "arrested" (stopped) onset of the disease, then logically researchers would be optimistic about new treatments.

6. B

Think very carefully about what this sentence is saying. There's no transition to tell you the relationship between the information before and after the semicolon, so you have to work it out on your own. Start with what you do know: the information after the semicolon tells you that it is tap choreographers that are *rare*. In context of the first part of the sentence, the implication is that astonishing solo dancers are *not rare*. So the first part of the sentence must express the *idea* that solo dancers are easy to find. But careful with the word "seldom" (rarely): even though the sentence must mean that solo dancers are common, the answer itself must mean the opposite (solo dancers are easy to find = solo dancers are seldom **hard** to find).

(B) is correct because "wanted for" means "needed," which makes sense in context: the field of tap dance has rarely needed dancers because there are a lot of them, unlike tap choreographers, who are unusual. "Scoffed at" (mocked, disdained), "inquired about," "tended toward," and "wavered about" (was indecisive about) do not mean "needed," so they do not fit the sentence. Even if you think that the correct answer sounds very strange in context, remember that how a word or expression *sounds* is entirely irrelevant – the only thing that counts is the meaning, whether or not it is familiar to you.

Set 36 (p. 71)

1. B

The key words "planted" and "staple crop" let you know you're talking about growing the rice, so "grown" or "farmed" would be a good word to plug in the blank. "Isolated," "retained" (held back), "confiscated" (stolen), and "multiplied" aren't synonyms for "grown" or "farmed," but "cultivated" is, so (B) is correct.

2. D

The second part of the sentence defines the blank: each province appointing its own ruler is a sign of independence, so you want a word that means something like "independence." "Humility" (being humble), "diligence" (being hardworking), "confidence," and "revenue" (money earned) all do not fit.

3. A

The sentence compares events that occurred in the twentieth century to events that occurred hundreds of years earlier. The first part of the sentence talks about unearthing objects (literally, pulling them out of the earth), which tells you that the word in the blank must have a similar meaning. Try plugging in something like "digging up." (B), (D), and (E) clearly don't make sense, and you can make an educated guess that "defiling" is negative because of the prefix DE-, not. "Excavating" is a synonym for "unearthing," so (A) is correct.

4. A

The word "while" indicates a contrast, so the second blank must mean the opposite of "preserved intact." You could plug in something like "incomplete." "Consolidated" (brought together) is the opposite of this, so cross out (C). "Unexceptional" means "ordinary," which also doesn't fit, so eliminate (B). "Euphonious" (pleasant-sounding, EU-, happy + PHON-, sound) is related to music but unrelated to being incomplete, so eliminate (D). And "despondent" means "depressed," which makes no sense, so eliminate (E). "Fragmentary" means "existing in fragments (pieces)," which fits as the opposite of "intact" (whole), so (A) is correct.

5. E

The construction "not as a…but rather" sets up contrast between the first and second blanks, so you know you're looking for a pair of antonyms. Start by looking at the relationship between each pair of words. (A): "negation" has nothing to do with "ephemeral" (short-lived). (B): "reaction" has nothing to do with "elemental" (fundamental). (C): "characteristic" has nothing to do with "acceptable." (D): "defense" has nothing to do with "illusory" (imaginary). (E): "diversion" (distraction) is the opposite of "integral" (essential). If you're still not sure, think about what the sentence is saying: the author regards poetry as a central part of his work rather than something that distracts from his work.

6. C

The key word is "instead," which indicates that the word in the blank will mean the opposite of having fixed settlements. "Peripatetic" (wandering) fits that definition, so (C) is correct. "Cordial" (polite), "sycophantic" (servile flattery), "dogmatic" (rigidly adhering to a belief), and "duplicitous" (deceptive) all do not make sense in context.

7. B

Start with the second blank. Genetically engineering apples would be contrary to wholesome and natural, so "destroy" would be a good word to plug in the blank. The correct word might not be that strong, but that's the idea you're looking for. "Admonish" (scold), "bolster" (improve), and "dominate" clearly don't fit with the clue, so cross off (C), (D), and (E). For the first blank, the sentence sets up a contrast: since the second half is negative, the first half must be positive. Since "not… _____" is positive, the word in the blank should be negative. "Interrogates" (questions intensely) doesn't fit, so (A) is out. "Compromises" means "makes vulnerable" which works, and "undermine" (subvert, ruin) works for the second blank, so (B) is correct.

8. E

"Scorned" (looked down on) and "only write about what they know" tell you that the word you're looking for must be negative and mean something like "self-centered." "Pedantry" (being knowledgeable but boring, irritatingly obsessed with minor details) is definitely negative, but it doesn't have to do with writing what you know, so (A) doesn't fit. "Sophistry" (making false arguments) and "obfuscation" (making things unclear) are negative but also don't fit the clues, so eliminate (B) and (C). And "profundity" (being profound) is positive, so eliminate (D). That leaves (E): look at the root SOL-, alone, as in "solitude:" "solipsism" is the belief that the self is the only thing that matters, so (E) is correct.

Set 37 (p. 72)

1. B

The key phrase is "the first book:" the word in the blank must be consistent with the idea that the book accomplished something *new*. That is the definition of "groundbreaking," so (B) is correct. Careful with the other answers: they might sound plausible because they're related to

books, but they don't fit the sentence. The book might also be eloquent (well-expressed), but that's not what the clue says, so cross off (A). It was actually a controversial book, but again, you're looking for a word that fits the clue, not just one that describes the book, so eliminate (C). "Meticulous" (carefully done) and "comprehensive" (all-inclusive) also don't fit the clue, so (D) and (E) are out as well.

2. B

The colon after "function" indicates that the second half of the sentence will explain the first half and define the two blanks. Think about parallel structure here: the first explanation defines the first blank ("chronicled tribal legends"), and the second explanation ("exchanging goods") defines the second blank. "Literary" fits with stories and legends, and "economic" works with exchanging goods, so (B) is correct. The other answers have nothing to do with either blank.

3. C

The key words "prohibitively expensive" indicate that paper cost a lot of money, so the word in the blank must be consistent with that idea. (C) directly corresponds to the idea of costing a lot of money – that is essentially the definition of "luxury." Careful with (D) and (E): although printing was an innovation (a new invention) during the age of Shakespeare and Milton, the word in the blank describes *paper*, not printing, and the sentence says nothing about printing being *new*. A commodity is simply something that can be used for trade or exchanged for money – it has a neutral connotation, whereas "luxury" is by definition expensive. An "implement" is a tool or piece of equipment, and a "concession" is the act of giving in, so neither (A) nor (B) is correct.

4. A

The key phrase "making small talk and cracking jokes" defines the word in the blank. That is the definition of "bantered" (chit-chatted), so (A) is correct. "Commiserated" (sympathized, CO-, with + MISER- as in "miserable"), "sauntered" (strolled), "circulated" (walked around), and "indulged" (gave into) all do not fit.

5. C

The sentence indicates that infrared light cannot currently be used by solar panels, so logically, a cell that could harvest infrared light would help the sustainable industry quite a bit. The word in the blank must therefore be positive and mean something like "help." A "harbinger" is a warning, which doesn't fit, so eliminate (A). "Rationale" (reason), "dichotomy" (contradiction), and "regression" (backsliding) all don't make sense either. A "boon" is a "benefit," which fits with the idea of helping, so (C) is correct.

6. E

If William argued with his friend, then logically his friend was angry, and he would try to calm her down. So fill in something like "calm" for the first blank. "Placate," "pacify," and "mollify" all fit that definition, but "conjure" (evoke or make something appear) and "castigate" (criticize harshly) don't fit, so eliminate (B) and (D). Now look at the second side: the fact that William's attempts to calm his friend were *futile* (in vain) tells you that they didn't work, and the word "in fact" tell you that they did exactly the opposite. So you're looking for a negative word that means "made worse." "Mitigated" (lessened) doesn't make sense in context because the friend's irritation didn't *decrease*, so eliminate (A). "Curtailed" means "stopped," so (C) doesn't work either. That leaves (E): "exacerbated" means "made worse," so that is the answer.

7. D

The key phrase "undisputed world language" tells you that you're looking for a word that means something like "total domination." That is the definition of "hegemony," so (D) is correct. "Ambivalence" (having mixed feelings),

"dichotomy" (apparent contradiction), "diatribe" (rant), and "vernacular" (dialect spoken by people in a particular region) all do not fit.

8. E

"Unable to comprehend" is a clue telling you that the blank will mean something like "incomprehensible." That is the definition of "opaque" (note the second meaning – it is more commonly used to describe an object that light can't pass through). "Impenitent" (unrepentant), "recondite" (arcane, obscure subject matter), "candid" (open, honest), and "deviant" (abnormal) all do not fit. Careful with (A) and (D): both are words commonly associated with criminals, but neither fits the definition that the sentence requires.

Set 38 (p. 73)

1. D

The word "although" sets up a contrast between the first blank and the second blank. For the second blank, the key phrase "a series of unexpected plot twists" indicates that the word in the second blank must mean something like "guess." Working from that information, the first blank must mean something like "obvious." If you start with the first blank, you can cross off everything except (A) and (D) immediately since "trite" (clichéd) and "predictable" are the only words consistent with "obvious" (if you don't know what "trite" means, you should leave it). Looking at the second side, only (D) makes sense since "foresee" has a similar meaning to "guess." If you worked from the second blank, you could immediately eliminate everything except (B) and (D), and "entertaining" clearly does not make sense, again leaving (D).

2. A

The sentence describes the grapefruit as a cross between two other fruits, so you're looking for a word that describes a combination or blending. A "hybrid" is a combination of two things (think of a hybrid car, which runs on both gas and electric power), so (A) is correct. "Temperate" means "moderate," and though a grapefruit might grow in a temperate climate, that's not what the clue is telling you the word must mean. "Ubiquitous" means everywhere, which also doesn't fit. "Culinary" means "related to cooking" and while a grapefruit is a food, the word doesn't fit the clue, so eliminate (D). "Exotic" is also tempting, but again, this word also has nothing to do with mixture.

3. A

The key words "even at the risk of" indicate that word will be negative. Since the sentence mentions Epstein "say[ing] precisely what he thinks," a good word for the blank might be "offending" or something similar. "Selecting" and "impressing" clearly don't fit, so eliminate (D) and (E). "Mollifying" (calming, MOLL-, soft) is the opposite of what you want, so eliminate (B). In (C), Epstein's friends could *become* offended if he satirized them, but "satirized" doesn't actually *mean* "offended." "Antagonizing" (angering, ANT-, against) is a much better fit, so (A) is correct.

4. C

The key phrase is "utterly drained of emotion," which defines the word in the blank. "Catharsis" refers to the emotional exhaustion that results from witnessing an intense spectacle or performance, so (C) is correct. "Tedious" (tiresome, boring), "bombastic" (pompous, pretentious) "ineffable" (inexpressible), and "clandestine" (secret) all do not fit.

5. C

Since Abelard "chose to study philosophy instead," he must not have pursued a military career, so try filling in a negative word like "rejected" for the blank. Eschewed means "rejected" so (C) is correct. "Contemplated" (thought about), "stipulated" (required) and "commended" (praised) clearly do not fit, so eliminate (A), (B), and (E). Careful with (D):

"defer" means "put off doing," but the sentence says nothing about Abelard coming to back to a military career *later*, so that doesn't work.

6. D

The key phrase "exaggerated gestures and unrestrained shows of emotion" indicates that the word in the blank must fit that definition. That is what "histrionic" (hysterical, over-the-top) means, so (D) is correct. "Authentic" (real), "ironic," "credible" (believable), and "cloying" (overly sweet) do not fit.

7. A

The construction "not only…but also" tells you that the words in the blanks must have similar meanings, so start by looking at the relationship between each pair of words. (A): "coincided with" and "linked" are similar, so keep it. (B): "relied on" is the opposite of "inured" (unaffected), so eliminate it. (C): "Deviated from" is the opposite of "bound," so eliminate it. (D): "borrowed from" is similar to "attracted," so keep it. (E): "railed against" (protested) is the opposite of "partial to" (liking), so eliminate it. If you're not sure how to choose between (A) and (D), think of it this way: architecture can't be "attracted" to anything, so (D) doesn't make sense. That leaves (A), which fits. It conveys the idea that Baroque architecture is usually associated with Europe, but it also had something to do with colonialism; the two things arose at the same time (coincided with) and were related (linked) to one another.

8. C

The fact that the author is "rarely explicit" means that it's probably hard to figure out what he really believes. So for the first word, you're looking for something similar to "beliefs," while for the second, you're looking for something negative like "prevents." Start with the second blank since it's a little more straightforward. "Inhibits," "forestalls," and "precludes" all mean "prevents," so keep (B), (C), and (E) but you can eliminate (A) and (D) because "reiterates" and "belies" (contradicts) don't fit. Now look at the first side: you're looking for a word that means "beliefs." "Prerogatives" (special privileges), and "incentives" (enticements) don't fit, so eliminate (B) and (E). That leaves (C): "convictions" are beliefs (note the second meaning), and "forestall" means "prevent."

Shortcut: When "conviction" appears in an answer choice, it's usually correct. Start by plugging it in to see if it works.

Set 39 (p. 74)

1. D

The sentence contrasts "common origin" with the blank, so try filling in a word like "different." Two things that are "distinct" are separate, so (D) is correct. Playing process of elimination, "contrived" (artificial), "theoretical," "established" and "incomprehensible" simply have nothing to do with being separate.

2. B

The key phrase "1,200 known species" lets you know that there is a lot of variety among the skinks, so plug in "diverse" or a similar word for the blank. That should get you to (B) immediately. "Territorial," "fascinating," "dangerous" and "exotic" are all words that *could* be used to describe lizards, but none directly fits the definition that the sentence requires.

3. E

The key phrase "unable to acknowledge its flaws" tells you that these proponents have an extremely (excessively) positive view of string theory. "Enamored with" (passionate about, look at the root AMOR-, love) is the only answer that conveys that idea. "Perplexed," "disturbed," and "opposed" are all negative, eliminating (A), (B), and (D), and "accustomed" does not fit with the idea of loving something so much that you can't see its flaws, eliminating (C) as well.

4. E

In order for a larger collective to form, many smaller groups would have to join together, so the rivalries would have to become less important or even disappear entirely. "Quelled" means "put down" or "suppressed," so (E) is correct. "Displayed" and "anticipated" simply do not fit, and "emboldened" is the opposite of what you want. "Chastised" (scolded) also does not make sense – even though the members of the groups might be scolded, the rivalries would actually need to *stop* so that the larger collective could form.

5. E

The key phrase "works of art in their own right" tells you that you want a positive word that means something like "masterpieces." "Paragons" are perfect examples, so (E) fits. "Compilations," "forerunners" (something that precedes the existence of another thing), "amalgams" (objects or ideas composed of parts taken from different sources) and "attributes" (characteristics) all do not have the definition that the sentence requires.

6. B

The key word "disappointingly" tells you that the first blank is negative. Eliminate (A) and (E) because "seductive" and "astute" are both positive. Now look at the second side. The key phrase "in contrast" indicates that you need a negative word meaning the opposite of the first word. Eliminate (C) and (D) because "nebulous" (vague) and "insipid" (boring, unoriginal) are negative. That leaves (B): "pedestrian" means "unoriginal," and "lucid" means clear.

7. C

The key word "enthusiasm" tells you that the professor had a very positive attitude toward her subject – if students with no prior interest in it were engaged (i.e. their interest was piqued), they must have picked up their enthusiasm from her. Although "infectious" is a word that is commonly associated with disease, here it has a positive connotation – it simply indicates that the student "caught" the enthusiasm from the professor. "Evanescent" (short-lasting), "gratuitous" (excessive, unnecessary), "seditious" (rebellious), and "intractable" (stubborn) all do not fit.

8. E

Start with the second blank since you have more information about it. The fact that the voters *resent* the policy tells you they have a negative attitude toward it, so if they "find it _____," that blank must be negative. "Adaptable" is positive, so eliminate (C). Now look at the first blank. If the government is eliminating services, the first blank must have to do with not spending money. "Oscillation" (wavering, being indecisive), "augmentation" (increasing, improvement), and "indulgence" (doing something pleasurable but potentially harmful) do not fit, so eliminate (A), (B), and (D). "Austerity" (spending money only on things that are absolutely necessary) fits, as does "objectionable" (unlikeable) so (E) is correct.

Set 40 (p. 75)

1. C

The key word "but" indicates that the word in the blank will mean the opposite of "near extinction" and will be positive. Try plugging in something like "growth." "Resurgence" is the word most consistent with that idea (RE-, again + SURGE-, increase), so (C) is correct. If you don't know what "resurgence" means, however, you can eliminate (A) and (E) because "collapse" and "reluctance" are clearly negative. "Modification" (change) is neutral and clearly

doesn't fit with the clue, so you can eliminate (B) as well. Careful with (D): it is true that bison might be easier to detect now, but you're looking for a word that means "growth," and that is not the definition of "detection." Which leaves (C).

2. E

The information after the colon defines the blank – the word must mean "someone who did not serve in the military." That is the definition of "civilian," so (E) is correct. Careful with (A): a commander is a role occupied by someone on a space flight, but it does not fit the definition provided by the sentence. "Itinerant" (wanderer), "mediator" (someone who helps two conflicting sides resolve their differences), and "ingénue" (in theater, the part of a young, innocent girl) all do not make sense.

3. A

The sentence contrasts a single industry with a _____ of fields, so the blank must mean something like "large number." "Plethora" means "abundance," so (A) is correct. "Derivation," "recapitulation" (summary), and "sequence" all do not fit, and "scarcity" is the opposite of the word you're looking for.

4. C

If Steven Joyce is "intensely suspicious" of biographers, then clearly he's going to have a negative attitude toward them. The word in the blank must therefore be a negative word that means something like "block" or "get in the way of." That is the definition of "thwart," so (C) is correct. "Augment" (increase), "engage," "contemplate" (think about), and "peruse" (examine closely) are all positive and do not fit the sentence.

5. C

Start with the second blank. "Reason" and "creativity" are positive, so you can cross off anything negative. "Detriments" means "bad qualities," and "enigmas" are mysteries, so (B) and (E) are out. Since the first blank is associated with a "goal" as well as "reason and creativity," you can assume you're looking for a positive word. "Exculpating" (freeing from guilt) is positive but does not make sense in context, so eliminate (A). "Winnowing" means "removing impurities or negative elements," so (D) doesn't make sense. (C), "endowing" means "granting," and "faculties" is a positive word used to refer to the senses or higher-level cognitive abilities (e.g. the faculty of reason) so (C) is correct.

6. D

The sentence contrasts the "tendency to _____ his poor health" with how van Gogh actually felt: deeply frustrated. So the first blank must somehow describe making his health seem good, or at least not frustrating. "Excoriate" (harshly criticize) is negative, so eliminate (A). "Palliate" (soothe) and "invigorate" (energize) might be tempting because those are things that would logically be done to someone in poor health, but neither makes sense in context. Eliminate (B) and (C). If you know van Gogh was an artist, "illustrate" could be tempting, but it has nothing to do with the sentence, so eliminate (E). "Romanticize" his poor health (make it seem romantic and exciting when it really isn't) is a much better fit for what modern critics would do, so (D) is correct.

7. C

The key phrase "used in herbal medicine" tells you that aloe vera is being used as a treatment, so you're looking for a word that means something like "treatment." "Virtue" doesn't match this definition, and neither does "deficiency" (lack), so cross off (A) and (D). Since aloe vera is presented positively, you can assume that the word in the first blank will be positive as well. "Harangued" (harassed) and "jettisoned" (threw away) are negative, so eliminate (B) and (E). In (C), "touted" means "praised," and panacea means "cure-all," so (C) is correct.

8. A

The key word "foreseeing" (seeing something before it happens) tells you that you're looking for a word that means "able to make predictions." That is the definition of "prescient" (PRE-, before, + SCI-, know), so (A) is correct. "Irreverent" (joking), "enervating" (tiring), "obdurate" (stubborn), and "beguiling" (charming) all do not fit.

Set 41 (p. 76)

1. A

The sentence tells us that the source "so _____ that *no one* initially noticed it," indicating that the word in the blank must mean something like "unknown." That is the definition of "obscure," so (A) is correct. "Extensive," "optimistic" (believing things will work out for the best), and "deft" (skillful) have nothing to do with being unknown, and "distinguished" is exactly the opposite of what you're looking for.

2. E

Even if you don't know that cuneiform is a type of ancient writing, you can make an educated guess since *archaeologists* are trying to figure it out. Logically, the first blank must mean something like "understand." For the second blank, the key phrase "*Although* archaeologists have made many attempts" indicates that the archaeologists have been unsuccessful at understanding the cuneiform. The second blank must therefore mean something like "puzzled." Start with the first blank: if you can recognize that "decipher" (DE-, not + CIPHER, code) is the only general synonym for "understand," you can plug in the other side and see that "confounded" (extremely puzzled) works as well because it is a synonym for "puzzled."

Careful not to get sidetracked: "display" and "excavate" (dig up) are both words that could easily appear in the same context as archeologists, but they have nothing to do with the clues in the sentence. (B) makes no sense because "evade" means "avoid," which is the opposite of what archaeologists would want to do with hieroglyphics. (D) doesn't make grammatical sense: you can determine the *meaning* of hieroglyphics, but you cannot determine hieroglyphics themselves.

If you were to work from the second blank, you could immediately eliminate everything except (B) and (E), and "evade" cannot be correct for the reason discussed above.

3. D

The key word "against" and the phrase "never been published in their entirety" indicate that the blank must be a negative word like "prohibition." If you don't know what an embargo (prohibition) is, play process of elimination; be careful with (A), (C), and (E) because an "anthology," "tome" (volume), and "abridgment" (shortened version) are all related to books but have nothing to do with the sentence. Be careful with (B) as well – a eulogy is a speech of praise given at a funeral, but the sentence only mentions the author's *will*.

4. E

This sentence sets up a similarity between the two blanks: the first is "merely difficult," while the second is "virtually impossible," so the second will be a harsher or more extreme version of the first. "Enable" and "deter" are opposites, so (A) is out. "Prosecute" and "recommend" are unrelated, so eliminate (B). "Denounce" (note the negative prefix DE-) and "replicate" (copy) are closer to opposites than synonyms, so (C) is also wrong. Prevent and encourage are exact opposites, so eliminate (D). "Restrict" and "contain" both have similar meanings, so (E) is correct. If you still don't quite get it, think about what the sentence is saying: in the past, it was difficult to stop copyrighted material from being distributed, but the Internet has made copyrighted material so easy to distribute that it is virtually impossible to stop it from being distributed.

5. B

The blank is paired with "detached," telling you that you're looking for a word with a similar meaning. That is the definition of "aloof," so (B) is correct. "Obstinate" (stubborn) doesn't work. Neither does "charismatic" (charming), so (C) is out. "Infallible" (unable to be wrong, IN-, not + FALL-, error) and "sycophantic" (servile, flattering) also don't work as synonyms for "detached."

6. C

The key phrase "examples…that instruct its readers" indicate that the word in the blank must have something to do with teaching or instruction. "Didactic" means "intended to teach," so (C) is correct. "Loquacious" (talkative, LOQ-, speech), "ambiguous" (unclear), "droll" (dryly amusing), and "vivid" (striking) are all unrelated to teaching.

7. E

The sentence contrasts "nuanced and passionate characterizations" with the two blanks, which must express the idea that the actress's characterizations no longer have these characteristics. The blanks are expressing a negative *idea*, but be careful: although you need a negative word for the first blank, the negation "devoid of" (lacking) before the second blank tells you that you need something positive. Start with the first blank: "ebullient" (enthusiastic) is clearly positive, and "subtle" is a synonym for "nuanced," so eliminate (A) and (C). Now look at the second side – remember, you need something positive. "Belligerence" (aggression) is negative, so eliminate (B). "Sonority" (having a full or loud sound) doesn't fit the clues. "Conviction" works because it is a synonym for "passionate" (devoid of conviction = lack of passion) and "generic" means generalized, run-of-the-mill – the opposite of nuanced (specific).

8. E

Since Munch is blurring the line between "originality and _____," you can assume that the word in the blank will means the opposite of "originality." Working backwards from that information, you can assume that Munch used outside influences in his art, so the word in the first blank must be consistent with the idea of using outside influences.

Start with the second blank since you have a little more information about it. "Verisimilitude" (truth), "profundity" (depth – the noun form of "profound"), "candor" (openness, directness), and "iconoclasm" (groundbreaking-ness) have nothing to do with a lack of originality, so you can eliminate everything except (E). "Synthesized" mans "brought together," which fits the idea of using outside influences, and "mimesis" means "copying" (think of "mimic"), so (E) fits.

Set 42 (p. 77)

1. D

The key phrase "introduced his ideas to a wide audience and made him a household name" tells you that Churchill's writings were a very *important* part of his politics. "Significant" means "important," so (D) is correct. "Legible" (readable), "discerning" (able to perceive small details), "courageous," and "deleterious" (bad) all do not fit.

2. E

The key words "one that" tell you that the two parts of the sentence are talking about the same idea and that the two words will have similar meanings. It's not absolutely clear from the sentence what either word must mean, so start by plugging each pair in. (A): an "elaborate" (detailed) model does not "exemplify" interaction, so eliminate it. (B): an "innovative" (new) model does not "attenuate" (weaken) interaction, so eliminate it. (C): a "defensive" model does not "encourage" interaction so

eliminate it. (D): a "communal" (shared) model does not "dissuade" interaction, so eliminate it. That leaves (E): a "collaborative" model is one in which people work together, so by definition it would "encourage" interaction.

3. C

The fact that reporters "continued to work there until authorities _____ the building" tells you that the word in the blank must mean something like "took over" or "closed down." "Commandeered" means "seized control of," so (C) is correct. "Vanquished" (defeated), "surveyed," "ascertained" (made certain of), and "investigated" all do not fit. Careful with (B) and (E): authorities may have "surveyed" or "investigated" the building, but the fact that the reporters could no longer work there tells you that the word must go further and convey the idea that the building could no longer be used.

4. A

The information after the colon tells you that Dickens' family was very poor. "Penury" means "poverty," so (A) is correct. "Solitude" (being alone, SOL-, one), "temperance" (not drinking alcohol) and "penitence" (repentance) do not make sense, and "affluence" (wealth) is the opposite of the word you're looking for.

5. E

"Time-consuming" is the key word, so you want a word that fits well with the idea of taking a long time. "Indecorous" (impolite) and "minimalistic" (bare, uncomplicated) don't work, so eliminate (A) and (B). For the first blank, you're describing a new method in contrast to the traditional, time-consuming method, so you want a word that conveys the idea of being fast or easy. "Extracted" (taken out; look at the prefix EX-, out) doesn't fit; neither does "associated." "Streamlined" means "made simpler," which fits perfectly, and "convoluted" (complicated) is a good match for time-consuming, so (E) is correct.

6. D

Start with the second blank. The sentence contrasts "completely reinvented" with "a less _____ approach." "*Only* if it were *completely reinvented*" is pretty extreme, so for the second blank, you're looking for a word that means "extreme." Think about what the sentence is saying: the fact that the festival has been successful recently suggests that it *isn't* necessary to completely reinvent it; an approach that isn't so extreme (i.e. a *less* extreme approach) would work just as well.

So for the second blank: if you know that you're looking for a word that means "extreme," you can jump straight to (D) because that is the definition of "radical." "Innocuous" (harmless) and "formulaic" (unoriginal) are more or less the opposite of what you're looking for, so (A) and (B) are out. "Contemporary" (current) doesn't make sense at all, and "partisan" (strongly adhering to a cause) doesn't quite fit – the opposite of partisanship is collaboration, and the sentence does not mention anything about working with other people. So (D) is the only possible answer, and when you plug "salvaged" (saved), it works as well: the festival could be saved with an approach that didn't involve overhauling the whole thing.

7. C

You have more information about the second blank, so start with it: the key word "ephemeral" (short-lived) tell you that the word must mean something like "ending." "Intensifying" (getting stronger) and "converging" (coming together) don't fit, so eliminate (A) and (E). For the first blank, heavy rains and high winds is a clue that this word will describe what the storm does. "Transgress" (do something forbidden) and "bypass" (go around) don't' fit, so eliminate (B) and (D). That leaves you with (C) – "blanket" means "cover," and "dissipating" means "disappearing," so (C) is correct.

8. C

For the first blank, "heavy-handed and lacking in _____" tells you that the word in the blank will be the opposite of heavy-handed (clumsy, forceful) so the word you're looking for must mean something like "delicacy" or "liveliness." "Significance" is positive but doesn't have quite the right meaning, and "ineptitude" means "incompetence," so eliminate (B) and (E). "Subtlety" and "nuance" are synonyms, and "aplomb" means "panache" or "liveliness," so (A), (C), and (D) work for the first blank.

Now look at the second blank: the word "although" indicates a contrast between the author's style (which we know is bad) and the questions he raises – if the style is bad, then the questions must be good. But careful! There's a negation: "this deficiency does *not* _____ the importance." So even though the idea is positive (the author's questions are important), the negation indicates that you need a negative word – two negatives make a positive. Try filling in something like "lessen" or "detract from." That is the definition of "trivialize" so (C) is correct. Both "legitimize" (make legitimate or legal) and "dignify" are positive, so (A) and (D) can be eliminated.

Set 43 (p. 78)

1. C

The key phrase "beginning college-level mathematics at the age of only thirteen" tells you that Jeffrey Sachs accomplished a lot academically very *early*, so you're looking for a word that captures that idea. "Precocious" fits because it refers to someone who can do things at an earlier age than other people. "Meticulous" (highly detailed), "inquisitive" (curious) and "versatile" (flexible) might also be words that apply to Sachs, but they do not fit the clue provided by the sentence. "Literate" (able to read) does not fit the sentence at all.

2. B

The key word "problem" tells you that each blank requires a negative word. Look at the first blank: "complex" is neutral and "buoyant" (able to float) is positive, so (A) and (E) can be eliminated. If you don't know "buoyant," however, you should leave (E). Now look at the second blank: "purification" is clearly positive, so eliminate (D). "Flimsy" (poorly constructed) doesn't make sense and is unrelated to "deprivation," whereas something "toxic" would logically "contaminate" groundwater. So (B) is correct. If you get stuck between (B) and (E), focus on "toxic," which is clearly negative and perfectly fits the sentence. It only matters that you know the definition of the correct answer.

3. E

The sentence makes it clear that getting too many of the first blank will lead to arrogance, so the first blank must be something positive like "praise" or "awards." "Demonstrations" wouldn't lead to arrogance, and neither would "hypotheses," or "critiques," so eliminate (A), (C), and (D). Now look at the second blank. This must be a positive word since it led to the scientists' original success. "Baseless" is clearly negative, so eliminate (B). "Novel" (new) makes sense in context as does "accolades" (praise), so (E) is correct.

4. C

In the first blank, the queen's powers being sharply _____ is contrasted with her influence over government policy, so you know you want a word like "reduced." "Exacerbated" (made more worse) is the opposite, and "assuaged" (calmed down) doesn't fit either, so eliminate (B) and (D). For the second blank, you're looking for something consistent with her influence over government policy, so "impeded" (prevented) doesn't work. "Prompted (caused) an influence" makes no sense, so eliminate (E). In (C), "curtailed" means "restricted," and "exerted (wielded) an influence" is a good contrast to that idea, so (C) is correct.

5. A

"_____ and obedient" is a clue that the word in the first blank must mean something similar to obedient. "Obstinate" (stubborn) clearly doesn't work, and neither does "intrepid" (brave) so eliminate (B) and (D). The contrast with the first blank and the phrase "poorly suited to life on a ranch" tells you that this word must mean something like "hard to handle." Although "docile" (tame) works, "indulgent" (overly lenient or generous) does not fit, so eliminate (C). In (E), "apathetic" (not caring) could almost work, but it isn't a synonym for "obedient," and "apprehensive" (nervous) isn't its opposite. "Timorous" means "shy," and "recalcitrant" means "extremely stubborn," so (A) is correct.

6. A

If East Germans were crossing the border into West Berlin, then they were going against immigration restrictions. "Circumvented" means "going around" (CIRCUM-, circle +VEN-, come) so (A) is correct. "Admonished" (scolded), "lauded" (praised), "debunked" (showed why a belief was false), and "expedited" (sped up) all do not fit.

7. C

The sentence is talking about a king, so logically he would want people to treat him with a lot of respect. In addition, the fact that he rewarded the ones "who were most _____" tells you that the two words will be synonyms. (C) fits because "sycophantic" and "obsequious" are synonyms meaning "servile" and fit with how a king would want to be treated. (A): "decorous" (polite) fits, but it isn't a synonym for "assiduous" (hard-working). (B): "ingratiating" (trying to get on someone's good side) fits, but it isn't a synonym for "capricious" (unpredictable). (D): "abstemious" (rejecting worldly goods) isn't a synonym for "effusive" (excessively enthusiastic). (E): "incorrigible" (can't be improved, IN-, not + CORR as in "correct") isn't a synonym for "solicitous" (caring).

8. B

The sentence indicates that Ruscha's artwork was *influenced* by the film industry, so you can assume that there will be a positive relationship between *Large Trademark with Eight Spotlights* and a movie screen. In addition, the sentence sets up a parallel between the two works mentioned after the colon, so you also know that the word in the blank will mean something similar to "evokes." "Defiant" (rebellious) and "exploitive" (taking advantage of) are negative, so eliminate (C) and (E). "Reverent" (deeply admiring) doesn't make sense because an artwork can't admire anything, so eliminate (A). "Contemplative" also doesn't make sense because an artwork also can't contemplate anything – it can only cause a person to contemplate it – so eliminate (D). (B) is correct because "redolent" means "reminiscent" or "evocative" – in other words, *Large Trademark with Eight Spotlights* evokes, or reminds viewers, of a move screen.

Set 44 (p. 79)

1. C

The key phrase "gentle and easy to train" tells you that the correct word will fit that definition. (C) fits with "easy to train" because an obedient dog is one that takes commands easily. "Impulsive," "vivacious" (lively), "morose" (sad), and "shrewd" (smart, cunning) all do not fit.

2. D

The key phrase "staunch unwillingness" is your only clue here. If the protesters and officials were "staunchly *un*willing" to do something, then the effects were almost certainly negative. So for the first blank, try plugging in something like "got worse." That means you cross off (B) and (C). If you're not sure about "vacillated" (wavered, was indecisive), keep it. Now think about the second blank. If the first blank is negative, then the second blank must be positive: being *un*willing to do something

positive usually leads to a negative outcome. Try plugging in something like "compromise" for the second blank. You can get rid of (A) because "offend" is negative. In (C), "improvise" (make up something on the spot) has nothing to do with compromising. In (E), "persist" doesn't make sense – if both sides were not willing to persist, then the confrontations would *decrease*. (D) is correct because if both sides did not negotiate, then logically the confrontations would get worse (escalate).

3. E

The words "so astounding" tell you that the results were unexpected or extraordinary: try "believed" or "imagined" for the blank. "Denied" doesn't fit; neither does "announced" or "protected." Be careful with (D): the fact that the results were extraordinary in no way indicates that they could not be *substantiated* (shown conclusively to be true). It simply indicates that they were difficult to believe. In this context, "conceived" is an exact synonym for "believed."

4. B

If thousands of visitors came to see him, Lonesome George must have been very popular. "An attraction" or something similar would be a good word to plug in for the blank. The sentence doesn't imply that George himself was an activist, so (A) doesn't fit. An epistle is a letter, which doesn't make sense at all, so eliminate (D). A paradigm is a model or example, which also doesn't make sense, so cross off (E). The second blank must describe what the tourists do – since they're coming to see Lonesome George, you can assume they have a positive attitude. "Foundered" means "lost their way," so (C) doesn't fit. In (B), "icon" fits with the idea of a big attraction, and "clamored" (shouted for, made an uproar over) works well in the second blank, so (B) is correct.

5. E

The sentence contrasts the blank with the fact that observers have tried to detect *tension* in Merkel and Steinbruck's relationship, so you're looking for a positive word that indicates *no* tension. Try plugging in "good" or "friendly." "Amicable" means "friendly" (AMIC-, friend), so (E) is correct. "Scandalous," "fractious" (argumentative), "acerbic" (biting, caustic), and "precarious" (fragile) are negative and do not fit.

6. E

The key word "hoped" indicates that the word in the first blank should be positive because people don't normally hope for something bad to happen. For the second blank, the key phrases "disappointed" and "its promises just as vague" indicates that the word in the second blank must be negative and mean something like "vague." So you're looking for a pair of opposites. If you know that "equivocal" means "vague" or "unclear," you can jump right to (E); "decisive" is the opposite of "vague," so that's the answer. Otherwise, play process of elimination. "Manipulative" is negative, but it doesn't mean "unclear," so eliminate (A). "Bureaucratic" and "corrupt" are often associated with bad governments, but neither means "vague," so eliminate (B) and (D). "Calculating" is also negative but has nothing to do with being vague, so (C) can be eliminated as well.

7. C

The word "but" tells you that the two halves of the sentence are expressing opposite ideas. The first half states that attractive designs that achieve widespread popularity risk becoming clichés, so logically, the second half of the sentence must express the idea that some attractive designs that achieve widespread popularity do *not* actually become clichés. The two blanks correspond to the two ideas in the first half of the sentence: the phrase "*succeed* in becoming" runs parallel to "*achieve* widespread

popularity," and the second blank runs parallel to "turning into a cliché."

The second blank is a little more straightforward – you're just looking for a word that means "cliché" – so start with it. "Banal," "trite," and "hackneyed" are all synonyms for clichéd, but you can eliminate (B) and (D) because "ludicrous" (ridiculous) and "coercive" (manipulative) don't fit.

Now look at the first side: you're looking for a word that has to do with achieving widespread success. "Conventional" and "understated" both have nothing to do with achieving success, so eliminate (A) and (E), but "ubiquitous" (being everywhere) fits. So the answer is (C).

8. D

The key phrase "the ease with which it shifts" tells you that you're looking for a word that means "able to easily shift." That is the definition of "protean," so (D) is correct. "Pedantic" (knowledgeable but dull, obsessed with small details), "decadent" (in a state of decline), "munificent" (generous) and "soporific" (inducing sleep) all do not fit.

Set 45 (p. 80)

1. C

The sentence contrasts the blank with "seclusion" (isolation), so you're looking for a word that means the opposite – try plugging in something like "well known." "Recognizable" provides an appropriate contrast, so (C) is correct. "Energetic," "permanent," "sympathetic," and "neglected" all do not fit as the opposite of seclusion.

2. B

The sentence equates the blank with abolishing government, so you're looking for a word that means "someone who believes in getting rid of the government." That is the definition of an anarchist (look at the root words AN-, without, and ARCH-, rule), so (B) is correct. "Democrat" clearly does not fit, so eliminate (A). An oligarch is one of a few wealthy rulers, so eliminate (C). A pragmatist is a practical person, so you can cross off (E). A conservative wouldn't want to get rid of the government (a very radical gesture), so (D) is also out, leaving (B).

3. A

The key phrase "for over a century" tells you that the word in the first blank will be relatively positive and have something to do with lasting for a long time. If you know that "enduring" means "lasting a long time," you can immediately identify it as the probable answer. If you're not sure, "potent" (powerful), "eclectic" (varied), and "idealized" (viewed as perfect) don't fit, so eliminate (B), (C), and (E). If you want to keep "permanent," look at the second blank: "defied" is negative, so eliminate (D). The phrase "continues to be" tells you that the second word will be positive as well. "Emulated" (copied) fits: if the production styles endure, then logically they are still being copied today.

4. C

The key phrase is "consistency of syrup:" syrup is thick and sticky, so you want a word that means something similar. "Translucent" refers to something that you can see through (TRANS-, through + LUC-, light), "aromatic" (think of "aroma," smell) means pleasant-smelling, "potent" (note the root POT-, power) means powerful, and "amorphous" means (shapeless, A-, not + MORPHE-, shape), so none of these words fit. "Viscous" means "thick," so (C) is correct.

5. A

You have more information about the second blank, so start with it. The key phrase "pushed the boundaries of musical design" tells you that that the word you're looking for means something like "revolutionary." A "recidivist" is a relapsed criminal, so (B) doesn't fit. A "lackey

is a servant, which lets you cross off (C), and a "charlatan" is a faker, so (E) also doesn't work. For the first blank, "disturbed a riot" doesn't make sense: a riot disturbs the peace, but a musical performance wouldn't disturb a riot. "Provoked" (set off) a riot does make sense, and an iconoclast is someone who goes against the established authorities, so (A) is correct.

6. B

For the first blank, the key words "so-called" are a clue that the scientists think this is not a revolution at all; in other words, it *isn't* original. So "deny" or "reject" would be good words for the first blank. "Explain" and "promote" clearly don't fit here, so cross off (C) and (E). The second blank is what the scientists *do* think, namely that the revolution is actually not very original. So you want a word that implies the same thing as what has come before. "Frustration" doesn't fit, and "rupture" is a break with tradition: exactly the opposite. Eliminate (A) and (D). That leaves you (B): "Deprecate" (look at the negative prefix DE-, not) means look down on, and "continuity" implies a lack of revolution, so (B) is correct.

7. C

The sentence contrasts "*ambitious* in scope" (positive) with the fact that the book "*fails* to offer a _____ argument" (negative), so you can tell that the word in the blank will be something positive that the book *doesn't* have. "Pervasive" just means common or found everywhere, so eliminate (A). "Disparate" means "containing conflicting elements," which doesn't fit at all, so (B) is also out. Moving on to the second blank, the words "but rather" tell you that the second word must be the opposite of the first. In (D), "scholarly" and "studious" mean almost the same thing, so (D) is out. In choice (E), "comprehensive" (all-inclusive) and "definitive" are both positive. (C) is correct because "coherent" (consistent) is the opposite of "motley" (varied, heterogeneous).

8. A

The information after the colon gives you the definition of the word – it must refer to something that changes dramatically and abruptly. "Mercurial" means "unpredictable," which is consistent with changing quickly, so (A) is correct. "Effusive" (enthusiastic, gushing), "obstreperous" (loud and noisy), "temperate" (moderate), and "anomalous" (unusual) all do not fit the idea of changing quickly.

ABOUT THE AUTHOR

A graduate of Wellesley College, Erica Meltzer has tutored the SAT since 2007, helping students raise their Critical Reading and Writing scores by hundreds of points. She is also the author of *The Ultimate Guide to SAT Grammar* and *The Critical Reader*. She lives in New York City, and you can visit her online at http://www.thecriticalreader.com.

Made in the USA
Columbia, SC
09 December 2023

28097585R00083